BREAKTHROUGH
PARENTING

Unlock the Secrets to a

Great Relationship With

Your Children

A. Jayne Major, Ph.D.

Deaconess Press

Minneapolis

Library of Congress Cataloging-in-Publication Data

Major, A. Jayne (Alta Jayne), 1937–
    Breakthrough parenting : unlock the secrets to a great
    relationship with your children / A. Jayne Major.
            p.   cm.
    ISBN 0-925190-69-1
    1. Parenting.   2. Child rearing.   3. Parent and child.   I. Title.
HQ755.8.M356   1993
649'.1 — dc20   93–38538
                                                                    CIP

Breakthrough Parenting © 1993 by A. Jayne Major.

Published by Deaconess Press (a service of Riverside Medical Center, a division of Fairview Hospital and Healthcare Services, 2450 Riverside Avenue South, Minneapolis, MN 55454). *Money Back Guarantee:* If after applying the techniques and suggestions found in this book, you are not completely satisfied with your purchase, please return *Breakthrough Parenting* to the Publisher for a full refund.

Cover design and interior page design by Tabor Harlow.

First Printing: November 1993.
Printed in the United States of America.

96   95   94   93   7   6   5   4   3   2   1

Publisher's Note: Deaconess Press publishes books and other materials related to the subjects of physical health, mental health, and chemical dependency. Its publications, including *Breakthrough Parenting,* do not necessarily reflect the philosophy of Fairview Hospital and Healthcare Services or their treatment programs.

For a current catalog of Deaconess Press titles, please call this Toll-Free number: 1-800-544-8207.

Dedication

THE PARENT CONNECTION, INC.

To the parents who made their "breakthrough" in the classes and
counseling sessions held at The Parent Connection, Inc.
Thank you for your trust and for proving that the skills and
knowledge in this book really do work.
We have grown together.

♥

Acknowledgments

This book would never have been written without my family. My husband, Joseph M. Major, who was my helper and mentor, and our adopted sons, Robert and Thomas Jay "TJ" Major. The experience of guiding them through their childhood years, to responsible adulthood, provided me with countless opportunities to make this book real.

I am so very grateful to the parents, staff, and those who served on the board of directors at The Parent Connection, Inc. in the last ten years. I am thankful to the perseverance and guidance of Robert D. Furber and Donald C. Tosatto who have served as presidents of the board of The Parent Connection, Inc. and to faithful members of the board, Dawn Clifton, Arthur E. Rubin, Barbara Newman, and numerous others.

Lawrence Hartstein and Richard Rossner and their beautiful wives, Kellie Hartstein and Rahla Kahn, and their children have taken the vision of training parents to new heights. Thank you for your enthusiastic support and good business sense.

The Inside Edge has been a continuous source and supply of fabulous friends who believe in going for your dream. Their inspiration and support has sustained me. My mastery coach, Tim Piering, has empowered me to achieve breakthrough and mastery in many areas of my life.

Dyane Mohr worked long hours and unstintingly gave her expert knowledge to pull together the pieces that became the first version of this book. Her enthusiasm was infectious. Ruth Halcomb lovingly polished the second version of the manuscript. Thank you, Colene Sawyer, for hosting the Writer's Edge and for your helpful suggestions; and Betty Greenberg, another Inside Edge friend, who took me to the American Bookseller's Association convention where this book proposal became noticed. Richard Baltin has been there each time I needed him for graphic and desktop publishing. His eye for detail and ability to capture an idea visually has been phenomenal. Thank you.

Jay Johnson, my enthusiastic editor at Deaconess Press, who patiently guided me to the completion of this book. Thank you. I am appreciative of the work of Ed Wedman for his contribution in getting the book published. Many thanks to Tabor Harlow for his cover and text design.

I am grateful for the friendship of Frances "Sparky" Sotcher, who also makes dreams come true at the Westside Vegetarian Community. My friend, Andrew Jay Gross, whose attention to detail, organization, and peace will surely lead us to a world beyond war. Thank you.

I am grateful for the teaching of Reverend Michael Beckwith at Agape, who has effectively introduced me to the "still, small voice" that has steadfastly led me on my life path.

There are others, too numerous to mention, who deserve to be included here. I love you all. I am blessed.

♥

TABLE OF CONTENTS

Dr. A. Jayne Major

PREFACE

Wouldn't it be wonderful if someone would write the ultimate book on parenting so that parents would know what to do in every instance? Unfortunately, that isn't possible. All I can do here is present general information, skills, and guidelines for what to do in situations you're most likely to encounter. Also, I could not be so presumptuous as to say to parents everywhere that I know all the right answers.

You, the parents, are the true experts. The judgment lies with you, and the right course of action is always dictated by the needs of each specific situation. But because the parenting experience has many commonalities, we can draw some valuable generalizations about the best thing to do in many instances.

In my experience, I've observed that all right-minded, sane parents want the same thing for their children: they want them to grow up to be responsible, loving, and confident adults; they want them to be good thinkers; and they want their children to experience a good life.

How can parents accomplish this goal? How can we instill responsibility in youngsters? We must first acknowledge that we, as parents, are the most important teachers of our children. Whether we realize it or not, we're teaching our children all the time, not only with what we say but with what we do. Few parents know how to use their power effectively to teach children what they want them to learn. None of us start out equipped with all that we need for the job of parenting. We all learn on the job, and learning means making mistakes. There's no such thing as a perfect parent. I certainly am not one, I don't believe I've ever met one, and I doubt that such a person exists. Making mistakes comes with the territory.

Fortunately, children aren't made of spun glass and most mistakes aren't tragic. Often we realize—after the fact—that we've done something wrong. This is an essential part of the learning experience. If you realize you're making mistakes, consider yourself lucky. You're one of the *aware* parents. Unaware parents make mistakes, sometimes serious ones, yet fail to see what's wrong.

The mistakes themselves aren't as important as what we do about them. That's what this book is about: understanding how to think positively so that we see ourselves as successful. When we're successful, we'll automatically be teaching our children that when they're responsible, they'll be successful, too.

My goal in writing this book is to share what I've learned about how parents can be effective role models and teachers of their children. The methods here are designed to help you become the most successful parent possible.

More Breakthrough Parenting

We are interested in hearing your breakthrough stories and concerns. How has this book worked for you? What questions do you still have? Share your family story with the rest of the world. If you have a story, poem, or article that you feel belongs in a future volume of *Breakthrough Parenting*, please send it to:

A. Jayne Major, Ph. D.
The Parent Connection, Inc.
Post Office Box 661212
Los Angeles, CA 90066

We'll make sure that you, as the author, are credited for the contribution. Thank you!

Yours in parenting,

Jayne Major
November, 1993

Please Note: You can also contact Dr. Major at the above address for speaking engagements or for information about her newsletter, parenting classes, other books, videos, audio tapes, workshops, and teacher training programs.

INTRODUCTION

"Just wait until you have kids!" No parent knows ahead of time what it will be like to be responsible for a child. When my husband and I first spoke with the social worker about adopting an older child, we talked about the kind of challenges we thought we could handle.

We had a lovely five-bedroom home in the suburbs. Both of us were working on doctorates in education at UCLA, and we both had long careers of teaching children. We believed that all children are beautiful and were ready to share our lives.

The social worker accommodated us quickly. Robert, nine, arrived on Mother's Day. He was grinning as he charged up the driveway with a pine cone in one hand and a paper sack full of ragged clothes in the other. He was an odd sight, with the sole of one frayed tennis shoe flapping as he walked. His hair stuck out in crazy directions, the result of a former neighbor's experiment in haircutting.

This sturdy fellow wanted to know, "Is it all right if I call you what I called my last mom and dad?"

"Why, yes, Robert. What did you call your last mom and dad?" I responded.

"Mom and Dad." With that, he marched in to check out his new home. He didn't notice my tears as I realized I was finally a "Mom."

Robert was quick to tell us what we wanted to hear: "I can't wait to start school." "Yes, I'll help out with chores." He assured us he could do almost anything around the house, and he agreed to a few routines we felt were important. That conversation was about the last time we agreed on anything for the next twelve turbulent years.

Robert was a very social person, so social he'd come home only for a quick pit stop or to sleep. He loved being with people, and our neighbors found him charming. We did our best to keep track of him, but he avoided being with us, even to eat. He knew the "soft touches" for food in the neighborhood. Although he would promise to tell us where he'd been, he rarely did. At dinner time, the perpetual question was, "Where's Robert?"

The times he was home for dinner, he didn't eat. He hated vegetables and almost everything else we ate. Having eaten elsewhere earlier, he wasn't hungry. He liked to sing, draw and daydream, especially when there were chores or homework to be done.

My husband and I were amazed at how much extra work there was keeping house with a nine-year-old boy around, and we felt it was good for children to be responsible for some of the housework. Robert, however, didn't agree. Once he was sitting by a small mountain of clothes that he hadn't folded for several days and sighed, "The reason people have foster children is so they'll do their work for them." That comment gave us some insight into Robert's thinking. This was "just another house" to him. His reasoning was understandable. Our house was his nineteenth move, and because of legalities, we wouldn't be able to adopt him for four more years.

Robert would lose almost everything, even the shirt off his back. When he felt hot, he'd throw his shirt on the ground and forget about it. We'd long since replaced his ragged clothes with durable new ones, but they were now rapidly disappearing.

In class, we learned that Robert would start an assignment, but after the first or second problem would trail off into singing, drawing, or daydreaming. He fumed at us for "making" him do things he didn't want to do. One night in bed, he glared at the ceiling with his arms resolutely crossed over his chest and declared, "I don't need parents!" He was twenty years old before he wavered from that position.

That incident started me thinking that our family wasn't complete with only Robert. TJ, Robert's younger brother, was still in a shelter home. Don't brothers belong together? We didn't know much about TJ, other than he was almost seven, so we asked the social worker to bring him by.

TJ arrived the next weekend, a strange little guy: hyper, swayback, skinny, and pot-bellied. He wouldn't look us in the eye, and he was clearly jealous of his brother's good fortune. As we watched them play, the social worker mentioned they didn't place the two brothers in foster care together because none of the foster parents could handle their fighting. When I asked about their background, I got only sketchy information. Their mother had been in jail several times. Their father wanted the boys adopted because they were more than he and his new wife could handle (together they had three younger children).

TJ moved into our home (his twenty-seventh move) one week later. After a single day of peace, the competition between the brothers exploded. While Robert fought with his fists, TJ fought with his mouth, the filthiest I'd ever heard. TJ was a master put-down artist, continually inviting negative attention. He was the exact opposite of Robert in that he couldn't get along with a soul, including us.

Fighting between the two brothers was incessant; their motto was "might makes right." For the first year, we didn't leave them in the same room with each other. My husband and I didn't have the stomach for the psychological and physical violence the boys were used to. Clearly, two gladiators had moved in with two pacifists. Our home was in utter chaos. We were rapidly approaching the proverbial "I've tried everything and nothing works!" stage.

As the boys entered adolescence, we saw how different our home was from the close-knit family we'd hoped for. In fact, our "family" wasn't working out. We didn't share the same interests or values at all. My husband and I loved school but the boys hated it. We loved classical and jazz music, but they liked hard rock at top volume. We believed in order and discipline while they would have none of it.

To make matters worse, we were unable to stop our teenage boys from taking dangerous risks. It was a frantic, chaotic time, the most stressful of my existence. I literally feared for their lives.

One day I exclaimed, "If it's this hard to be a parent, who trains parents?" This was a fateful question, for it marked the beginning of my new career.

I read popular how-to books on the subject. At first, they sounded like recipe books: if it looks good, try it! When I read more books, I saw that the experts disagreed on fundamental issues—punish, don't punish; praise, don't praise; exercise authority, have a democratic family. How could these "experts" disagree so strongly on how to raise children?

In my philosophy classes, I'd learned to ask, "Why? What could the solution be?" How could we help our sons overcome the abuse and neglect they suffered in their most formative years?

I needed to write a dissertation for my degree, and decided to research the parent's role. I read what the greatest minds said about raising children and about "What is the Good Life?" I finally chose to compare and contrast the three most popular approaches to raising children (humanism, democracy and behaviorism, well-espoused in the books *Parent Effectiveness Training (PET)* by Thomas Gordon, *Children: the Challenge* by Rudolph Dreikurs, and *Parents are Teachers* by Wesley C. Becker, respectively). After I figured out how to determine the goals and methodology, I concluded that the three approaches had serious problems, yet each offered valuable insights.

I applied these skills and concepts to handling the increasing problems my husband and I were having with Robert and TJ. It was becoming harder to communicate with them. They were undisciplined. Any efforts to punish them backfired as they found creative ways to punish us back, which led to further deterioration of our relationship.

Once my doctoral requirements were met, I needed to broaden my knowledge with the experiences of other parents. The maxim that people teach what they need to learn was true for me. I had two objectives: (1) to improve my relationship with our boys; and (2) to research what other parents needed to learn. Teaching parent education classes to different ethnic groups allowed me to help other parents while helping myself as a parent. My stories about the boys latest antics spiced up these early classes. The parents shared their wisdom and helped me through turbulent times. I realized that certain fundamentals of parenting exist in all cultures and in all people, rich or poor.

In the Westchester Adult Education classes, temper tantrums and potty training were the biggest issues. There were some parents of older children who rarely spoke in class. I was aware that their children had some trouble with the law and perhaps I was too polite to ask them for more information. It was clear they didn't want to volunteer anything too personal, so I didn't push. Each asked for a certificate of completion when they had attended ten classes.

I didn't know much about these parents until my own problems hit home. TJ was sentenced to juvenile hall for breaking and entering. I was devastated that he could have done such an antisocial thing, and at my own "failure" for not having prevented it.

I went to class as usual and as I stood in front of my seemingly well-adjusted parents, I felt I was anything but the parenting expert they thought I was. Scanning the room, I recognized that six of the parents were court-referred to the program. At the break, I asked them to go to the next room with me.

I started by saying flatly, "My son went to juvenile hall today for burglary." One mom said, "Mine too!" The seven of us came alive, each telling our own stories. When the break was over, I said, "We have to form our own group. Come to my office next Thursday night at 7:30." That night, in June 1983, The Parent Connection began.

Judge Roosevelt Dorn, a local juvenile court judge, kept these classes busy as he routinely sentenced parents of delinquent teenagers to parental guidance classes. (If TJ had him for a judge, I'd have been sentenced to my own classes!) The Department of Children's Services, Department of Probation, and The Child Advocacy Office all started referring the parents in child abuse and neglect cases. Soon the Los Angeles Police Department saw that we provided an excellent resource for desperate parents. When children had not been caught breaking the law, but were out of control, police officers would say, "Call The Parent Connection." The Police Department officials talked to the City Attorney's Office. When an anti-gang program developed, we were asked to train the parents of children in gangs. And a whole parade of parents who were facing jail time for their part in the juvenile delinquency of their children began attending class. I was amazed at how many domestic violence cases we were getting, too. These individuals were considered to be the "lightweight offenders," people who had no children but couldn't control their tempers with their significant others.

I was surprised at how much credibility I had with parents and the officials who were referring them to our classes. People said that they appreciated hearing from someone who had "been there." I confess that I was learning about what works along with them. I trained several teachers to do our "Skillful Parenting: Because Love is Not Enough" classes in both English and Spanish at numerous locations in Los Angeles.

Family law attorneys began to realize that they could strengthen their clients' cases in court if they had evidence of completing a series of parenting classes. Numerous fathers seeking custody or even visitation rights have also come to the program. I formed a special group for them, and they continued to come back, often for several years, to the "Fathers and Custody" class.

TJ had settled down after juvenile hall, but now it was Robert's turn. Robert had stopped trying. He was going to school intermittently and became more heavily involved in drugs. The leader of a local gang made friends with him, and he became consumed by their activities. My husband and I lost all control of him. This was a frightening time. I feared for Robert's life.

I called our adoption worker, Peggy York, to ask for advice. She said that Robert and TJ's birth father and his wife, John and Jackie, had called to inquire about the boys. Contact was established and it was arranged that Robert would move to Texas to stay with them. Jackie arranged for extensive therapy for him. We felt that Robert needed to leave the neighborhood, and needed to address some unfinished emotions about John. Robert was portraying his biological father as larger than life, or superhuman.

After spending a year living in Texas, Robert moved back with us. He was much improved from the therapy. He could look us in the eye and easily express his feelings. He also had empathy for other people—that was a breakthrough! He and I had many fascinating conversations about life. Many of them I'll always treasure. He was hardly cured, though. We were relieved that he was no longer interested in the gang and that his attendance at school was better, but he continued to avoid responsibility by using drugs as an escape.

In 1987, The Parent Connection, Inc. was incorporated as a nonprofit agency that specializes in parents who are in crisis and at high risk. We teach parents the fundamentals of responsible family life fifty weeks out of the year. Most of these parents are in legal trouble. Some have abused and neglected their children; some have teens in juvenile hall or probation camp or problems with domestic violence. Some have been referred from the City Attorney's anti-gang program. Others include fathers or mothers seeking custody of their children. Many of our parents are in turmoil as they pick their way through the legal maze. Their burden involves several costs: time, money, energy, and emotions.

Parents who walk through our door are furious, frustrated, guilty, miserable and in varying states of despair, yet the despair changes to hope in a remarkably short time. The Parent Connection's formula for success has enabled scores of parents to find fulfillment in their family life. Over 7,000 parents have completed these classes. More and more parents are interested in being trained as parents to prevent trouble. When people know better, they do better!

After just a few classes, I hear parents saying, "I wish that I had learned this years ago. I can't believe how much there is to learn." In the classes parents also discover they're not alone. They sympathize and provide support for each other.

How did they get into such trouble? Most parents do what their own parents did; many beliefs and traditions have been passed along for generations. Some parents still use techniques that were popular in the Dark Ages.

People once thought of children as objects or as personal property. They didn't recognize the importance of feelings and of treating children with dignity and respect. Cruelty was a way of life. Human rights as we know them did not exist.

Only since the middle of this century has child rearing been studied in depth. Great progress has been made in education, psychology, medicine, and nutrition. Phenomenal amounts of research have been accumulated. Some of the world's greatest minds have studied children. Swiss psychologist Jean Piaget (born in 1896), was known for his breakthrough discoveries in children's behavior and thinking. Harvard University's Lawrence Kohlberg studied the developmental stages of ethical behavior. Arnold Gesell (1898–1961), founder of the Gesell Institute, studied in detail the stages of children's growth. There have been so many scholars conducting research on children and the family that we can easily replace ineffective and damaging ways of raising children with positive methods that make our families a joy. *So much is known about raising children today, and too few people know about this key information!*

It is sad that many people learn how to parent so late in life. I see many good people who are bad parents. Outsiders think that parents who abuse and neglect their children don't love them. I've met these parents, and *I don't believe this!* The parents I've seen, even in the worst cases, are people who simply don't know what to do. They lack the fundamental skills and knowledge necessary for the job. If they knew better, they'd do better—and the same is true for their children. No one intends to make mistakes. It is easy to react without thinking through the consequences of our actions. This, and lack of training, can turn good people into bad parents.

My parents and grandparents were not trained to be parents. Were yours? The informal instruction we received from our families and their friends is the *most* training that parents ever receive for the *most* important job they'll ever have, that of raising the next generation. What a difference even a little training can make!

I'm fond of the saying, "If the only tool you have is a hammer, then every problem looks like a nail." In retrospect I can see that it takes many tools and considerable knowledge to raise a human being to adulthood. Once I made up my mind to take on the challenge, I wanted to equip myself with all the tools that are basic to doing the job. I needed to fine tune, change, and adjust these tools to suit the needs of our children as they were growing. I was certain my children deserved the best parents, and just as certain that in spite of my best intentions, I didn't know enough.

I thought that raising children would be easier than it was. I wasn't prepared for how much family life had changed since I was a child. The experiences my children were having were nothing like what I had experienced growing up. It was hard to appreciate how difficult it was for them to be in school, to conform to routines, and to adopt to standards that, while they seemed appropriate to us, were foreign to them. Life today is so complex that what once seemed natural no longer is.

I wrote this book because it is the book that I wanted to read when I was going through tough times. I also wish that I had known the contents of this book when my children were growing up. Yet, it is because of them that this book was written. I've seen how the "Skillful Parenting: Because Love is Not Enough" classes have helped so many parents. I believe that *Breakthrough Parenting: Unlock the Secrets to Having a Great Relationship with Your Children* includes the best our family traditions have to offer and the most up-to-date parenting information available.

I have no illusions that Joe and I have been successful in raising our sons to a well-adjusted, responsible adulthood. Looking back at my parenting experiences, I wish I'd been more patient. Now I understand more about the source of their unhappiness and problems. I realize that when children have been deprived in their early years, they'll be behind developmentally. My constant nudging for my children to be more mature, more aware, and more capable was inappropriate until they learned more of the basics. What parent doesn't reflect on what it would have been like from the vantage point of hindsight? I am, however, very pleased that Robert and TJ have taken charge of their lives and are finding their way to live what is a "Good Life" for them. They have more depth and understanding about life than many. It is a thrill to hear those lessons that I thought were falling on deaf ears, repeated back to me now. As young men, I see that they've caught up and are still growing.

And now we have another chance to be good role models and a positive influence on a child—TJ has made us grandparents. I'm certain my grandson, Tyler, will turn out perfectly!

"Hope springs eternal" is a popular saying in the Major family.

CHAPTER ONE

SO YOU'RE A PARENT...NOW WHAT SHOULD YOU DO?

Employment Opportunities

Wanted: One couple to procreate and raise a child. No experience necessary. Applicants must be available twenty-four hours per day, seven days per week, and must provide food, shelter, clothing, and supervision. No training provided. No salary. Applicants will pay out thousands of dollars over the next twenty-one years. Accidental applications accepted. Single persons may apply but should be prepared for twice the work.

—Author unknown

Job Description

Maybe you never thought of being a parent in quite this way before. The "job" requires an enormous commitment of time, energy, and money. Unfortunately, many parents figure out the job description about the time their grandchildren arrive.

Alone with Two Brats and All the Bills

Pat, a single mother, has all the financial responsibility for her two children and has little other support since her parents live far away. "I hate myself when I scream at Chelsea and Dirk. I hope no one will hear me. It's so ridiculous. Here I am screaming at my two stubborn kids as loud as I can and I'm embarrassed that someone might hear me. I feel stupid. My kids are brats. They won't listen the first, second, or third time I tell them to do something. If I really scream, they pay attention. There must be a better way. When I was their age, I minded the first time—why don't they?"

Pat may have a bit of amnesia about how well she minded as a child. She sees her mother-deaf children as stubborn brats, and they are living up to the label. She is worn out from trying too hard and still not getting results.

I Thought Having a Family Would Be Fun

Gerry dreads going home. He's already annoyed before he picks up Jennifer (5) and Jason (3) from day care. He waits while they get their belongings. In the car they are loud and, sure enough, Jason starts to whine, something Gerry hates. He's thinking, "I bet Sandra (10) is probably sitting in front of the TV instead of doing her homework or anything else to help out. She's selfish." Maxine, his wife, won't be home from work until 6:30. She gets the children off in the morning because he leaves so early. It's his job to manage the household at night.

Gerry thinks, "I thought having a family would be fun. I'm half dead and I've got to fix dinner. Maybe the children will go to bed on time, and Maxine and I can spend some time together. Will this mess ever get better?"

The Head-Cracking Mom and the Knife-Wielding Teen

Although Wanda told Tanika (15) to do the dishes at 6:00, Tanika is still talking on the phone three hours later. Walking away, Wanda realizes that she is not in control here. Tanika is. Not only that, Tanika puts up a fight over everything she asks her to do. How unfair it is, Wanda thinks, her anger rising. Tanika finally hangs up, but immediately begins to dial another number. Seething with rage, Wanda yells "Now!" As Tanika tries to wave her away, Wanda grabs the phone and without thinking, slams the receiver down on her daughter's head, which begins to bleed profusely. "I'll get you!" Tanika shrieks.

She disappears, returning just seconds later wielding a butcher knife. "Let go!" Wanda screams and tries to wrestle it from her. The knife clatters to the floor. Tanika, her face streaked with blood, gives her mother a cold, hard stare and threatens, "If you go to sleep tonight, you won't wake up tomorrow." Wanda feels a cold chill run through her body. She manages to take her other daughter, Sherryl (10) to her sister's. Sherryl, who has seen and heard all, is sobbing.

It was 10:00 P.M. on Sunday night when I got the call from Wanda. "What should I do? I'm terrified to go home."

Parent Burnout

What do Pat, Gerry, and Wanda all have in common? These parents are all miserable. They see themselves as failures and as victims of their own children. They're burned out. They don't know how to get their needs met in a family situation. Like so many parents, they lack basic skills in child care. They didn't learn parenting skills in their homes and they didn't learn them in school, but they finally learned what they needed to know at The Parent Connection.

Recently, I received an invitation to Pat's graduation from college. (Pat was the single mom with the two "brats.") Her children are now healthy, vibrant teenagers. Dirk, her eldest, is graduating from high school and plans to major in business at a local college. Chelsea, an A and B student, is also an accomplished gymnast.

Pat stopped screaming at her children after her first parenting class eleven years ago. On that same day, her children stopped living up to the label of "stubborn brats." She was highly motivated to learn better ways of parenting. She happily reported from week to week on how much more she was enjoying her children as she practiced the new skills and knowledge she had gained.

Gerry and Maxine (the hardworking parents of three children) came in for a private session. It was obvious that they had a strong relationship and had looked forward to having children, but now they were overwhelmed. I got them to relax, gave them some quick tips on organization and stress management, and sent them to parenting classes. Before the ten classes were up, they were enjoying their family life again and looked forward to weekend outings with the children.

Wanda, however, was another story. Her daughter, Tanika, ended up in juvenile hall and a nine-month camp program. I worked with Wanda for a long time. She was a quiet, soft-spoken person, yet she was sitting on an emotional powder keg. Her anger was just below the surface. She had never addressed the abuse she herself had experienced growing up. I helped her heal some old wounds. In the classes, she learned to be consistent and to control her violent reactions.

Meanwhile, Tanika calmed down. Both were distant from each other until Tanika was older. At eighteen, Tanika became a mother. The baby's father faded into the background and finally no one heard from him any more. Tanika needed Wanda's help. As trust developed, mother and daughter began to talk about their true feelings. There were no more violent episodes after that fateful Sunday mother/daughter assault.

The Importance of Parent Education

Think of a job that you do for pay. Consider how much training, time, energy, and expense you acquired to become good at that job. The manicurist that does my fingernails needed to have 300 hours of study, training, and observation to become licensed. But consider how few parents are ever formally trained in the most important job they'll ever have: raising children. Our society has not understood the importance of parent education. Good parent training can make us guilt free when we're in our families. Why? Because we can learn what to expect and how to handle problems as they develop without playing the punishing "blame game."

Human beings do not parent from instinct. This explanation is too simple. Dogs, cats, and hamsters have instinctual responses that tell them what to do. Many animals parent for a very short time before their offspring become independent. People, however, *learn* how to parent from others. Some confuse the intense love that they feel for their child as instinct. Human beings are complex. The society that we all have to adjust to is difficult to understand. The global community we live in is vast. Instinct doesn't explain how we raise our children to responsible adulthood.

Some people are more natural at parenting. Their parents or other caretakers were positive role models earlier in their lives. They may have been born with an even, unflappable disposition. They were more likely to have cared for younger brothers and sisters or other children, so they had more childcare experience to draw from. Sometimes our parents made very clear impressions about what *not* to do, classic negative parenting examples. There are many places where we learn to parent. Everyone has been exposed to this informal learn-from-direct-experience education.

The most that is known about how to raise children has been learned in the last half of the twentieth century. We now know the critical importance of protecting your child's self-esteem and developing his or her ability to think by "catch them being good" (more on that later). We also know the normal developmental stages that most children will predictably move through. More than parents in any other generation in history, you have the tools and the information to be a great parent, breaking through all the previous barriers and pitfalls.

Parent education can show you how to replace the dysfunctional methods that have turned children into the walking wounded. You may have to change centuries of inherited conversations that may not serve you and your family. It is by being trained as a parent that you can get a fresh start and develop the good habits that will make you more effective and certainly, ultimately, more successful. No one wants to abuse and neglect their children, yet it's done continuously. Why? It isn't because parents don't love their children, it's because they don't know a better way. When people know better, they do better. *Breakthrough Parenting* is the story of The Parent Connection, and it will teach you what parents have learned in those classes.

No one chooses to be in a family so that they can suffer, yet many people do. Everyone wants more pleasure than pain in their life. Pleasure comes from getting our needs met in a routine and comfortable way, and we rely on our families to do this. The families who have managed to get their survival needs taken care of are functional. Those that don't are dysfunctional. What is a need? Something that you have to have, like food, shelter, clothes, love and affection, money, safety, medical care.

But good parenting—breakthrough parenting—is about more than just meeting your family's survival needs. Everyone wants to live a *good life*, a life filled with an abundance of prosperity, harmony, love, and cooperation. We all want peace of mind. The Good Life springs forth out of family strength, predictability, flexibility, and the power of positive thinking. So let's find out the "secrets" that make this all possible.

Who's in Charge Here?

Now that you already have children, it's obviously too late to choose *not* to be a parent. What you can do , though, is learn to make the most of the experience. Start that positive process with this parenting secret—once you're a parent, you're in a position of authority, and this means you have *power*. An important measure of how well you perform your parenting job is how well you understand and use your power.

5

Expert

You may not be an "expert" in the sense of having formal training. Few parents are. But you have more knowledge, experience, and skills than your children. From a child's perspective you're the expert in what to believe and how to act. No one will have greater influence over your child than you. Your behavior is more important than what you say. What you *do* is the most decisive factor in teaching responsibility. A primary aspect of your job is to teach your child to know the difference between right and wrong and between fact and opinion. One of your major goals is to help your children understand how to have positive social values.

Official Position

As a parent you have an official legal and social role. You have a legal obligation to see that your children abide by the laws of your country, state, and community. Every state has laws on child care, and the rest of society depends on you to raise your children to treat themselves and others with respect and consideration. *We all want to be safe from each other's children.*

You also have an ethical obligation to treat your children as individuals who deserve dignity and respect. With this treatment, your children will be able to mature into responsible adults with their self-esteem and confidence intact.

Three Ways to Use Power

The power you have as a parent enables you to do three things: (1) to influence; (2) to reward; and (3) to punish, which means to do physical or psychological harm. Let's look at each of these.

Influence

To influence another means to give reasons advocating a certain point of view or to demonstrate ways of thinking or acting. The person being influenced is free to think or act differently. People usually change when shown a better way, but the reasons to change must make sense to them. Influence never implies forcing. The process allows the other person or persons to exercise free will.

Here is one example of parental influence in action. Frances notices Jessica (16) spending considerable time with a boy named Jerry. "Jessica, I know that you like Jerry very much. I'm worried about that. Jerry doesn't do well in school and his brother was arrested for dealing drugs last year. This autumn Jerry was expelled from school for smoking marijuana on campus. I hope you'll think this over and see if Jerry is the best kind of friend for you."

Frances states facts about Jerry in an attempt to influence Jessica. Frances wants Jessica to realize that he isn't a wise choice for her. Mom will want to follow through on this situation in a different way if the "influencing" technique doesn't work.

Reward

As a parent you have the power to use rewards. By using praise and other forms of approval, you can guide your children in their choices. This type of power isn't influence. It's a form of control using acknowledgment or other esteem-building incentives. The following example shows how rewards can help steer our children in the right direction.

When Chelsea was in seventh grade, she wasn't doing well in her classes, but Pat hoped that her winter quarter report card would show considerable improvement. Chelsea had a big smile on her face as she walked in the door with her report card. When Pat saw the grades, she smiled, too. "That's great, Chelsea! I'm so proud of how hard you worked to get these good grades. It shows that you're really paying attention to your school work. Let's celebrate and go to the movies on Saturday. You get to pick the movie. You deserve a treat for working so hard."

Pat uses liberal praise and encouragement with Chelsea. She also follows through with a reward for hard work. Wise parents rely more on influence, rewards, and discipline (which we will cover in a later chapter) than on force, punishment, or abuse. Earlier in the fall quarter, when Chelsea had Ds in math and science, Pat used a more disciplinary approach, she spoke assertively to her. "Chelsea, you must do better than this. It's your job to complete all of your assignments and hand them in on time. You're to write down how you plan to do this. Until we agree on this plan, you're to stay in the house."

Chelsea and Pat discussed the plan several times, and Chelsea confessed that she felt her science teacher hated her. Pat agreed to visit the teacher with Chelsea to see if this relationship could be improved. Pat also found a tutor for Chelsea to help her with math assignments. Pat and Chelsea worked together organizing study times. Throughout the process, Pat was supportive, yet firm. Making a plan and following through paid off.

Punishment

Punishment means to cause another person to suffer or to feel pain. There are two kinds of punishment, psychological and emotional. Parents must be careful when using pain as they exercise their parental power because it can backfire in a number of ways. Sarcasm or belittling the child is ineffective and destructive.

When Eileen's son, Rick, was 13, his grades were low. In an attempt to get him to do better, she embarrassed him and applied a harsh punishment. I've heard the results of this method far too often at The Parent Connection. Eileen's story is a classic illustration of *psychological punishment*.

"Rick, you're sure goofing off in English and math. How could you bring home such a bad report card? What's the matter with you? You can forget about after-school sports. You're grounded until you get a report card with As and Bs!"

No matter how hard he tried, Rick was unable to measure up to his mother's standards. He didn't understand math. He couldn't seem to get along with his English teacher. He got discouraged, then he started ditching school and sneaking out. Rick discovered that a lot of the guys in the neighborhood avoided the whole hassle by not going to school.

Because parents have considerable authority and power to coerce their children's behavior, they are often quick to use pain or punishment. When Ellen realized that Rick had stopped trying at school, she said, "Rick, if you don't get with it and do better in school, I'm going to send you to Texas to live with your grandmother. You're grounded for ten weeks until your next report card. You'd better smarten up before I buy you a one-way ticket."

Psychological intimidation relies on threats and the escalation of fear, and may be accompanied by insults as well. It's an excessive use of power. Rick's rebellion heightened, and he soon joined the Crips, a violent street gang in Los Angeles. Eileen's use of psychological punishment backfired tragically.

Other parents rely on the traditional "*board* of education." They believe in *physical punishment,* and that hitting a child actually teaches a good lesson. They may even be convinced that children "need" to be hit or they won't learn right from wrong.

Punishment means pain. How much pain is appropriate in disciplining a child is one of the most controversial issues in parenting. Too much physical pain leads to bodily injury. Mental trauma is a serious result of both psychological and physical punishment. Harsh punishment can undermine children's ability to use their intelligence and erode their self-esteem and confidence. In this way, many parents unwittingly cause their children to achieve far less than what they are capable of. When punishment is too severe, it creates frustrated, vindictive, uncooperative, and fearful children. Many parents fail to realize that insults or negative words can cause long-term psychological damage. And possibly the worst byproduct of negative parenting styles is that they're recycled from one generation to the next. Children who are punished harshly will tend to do the same to their own children. Using punishment to control children is one of the worst methods any parent can use. Now is the time to replace punishment with discipline. Robert and TJ are still struggling with their self-esteem du to the harsh punishment they received in their most formative years.

At The Parent Connection, we teach a variety of ways to discipline without forcing children to experience undue pain. This is another of our "Good Life secrets." Parents should rely more on influencing, rewarding, and disciplining children than on using force to get cooperation. If "this hurts me more than it hurts you," you're probably doing it wrong. When you're disciplining from love, the action you take doesn't feel bad.

Most parents think that they must protect their children from pain and suffering at the hands of another, yet they feel that it's their duty to punish a child who disobeys. They unwittingly fall into the role of being an oppressor and the child becomes a victim. Since pain and the stress it causes interferes with most learning, parents need more parenting tools.

When people know better, they do better! It's our job as parents to teach our children. The great teachers make learning something to look forward to, and the great teachers have one method in common. It's unbeliev-ably simple, yet it's one the most important secrets of successful parent-ing—catch your children being *good*.

CATCH
THEM
BEING
GOOD

There's no method in this book that has more significance and potential for success than the fundamental method of looking for and call-ing attention to what your children do right. When those parents who have been trained to think negatively finally get this simple concept, they can turn around 180 degrees and achieve a breakthrough in their family.

Too many people think that they are doing someone a favor by pointing out the errors of their ways. The problem is that negativity focuses on what *not to do* rather than on what *to do*. Negativity is the absolute destroyer of the Good Life that we all want to live.

Your job as parent requires that you be a leader. Much depends on the leadership style you choose and your sensitivity in using it. The most successful leaders of children are closely tuned into the importance of "catch them being good."

The following chart is filled with parenting secrets I'd like to share with you. It will help you understand the different qualities of the Most Successful vs. the Least Successful parent. One side comes primarily from a place of love; the other from a place of fear. It's worth taking the time to analyze how you feel about parenting most of the time. Are you constantly living in fear of what will go wrong next? Or are you fairly calm most of the time about what your children do? Remember that most parents do what their parents did to them—we only know what we know. Now is a good time to do some fine-tuning with your own parenting methods. You can choose to be a Most Successful parent right now. This choice is an impor-tant one for you to make, no matter what you grew up with or what kind of parent you've been to date.

The MOST Successful Parents Are:	The LEAST Successful Parents Are:
Warm and Accepting	**Rejecting and Hostile**
1. Satisfied with child's abilities and characteristics.	1. Not satisfied with child's abilities and characteristics.
2. Seeks out and enjoys the company of the child.	2. Doesn't seek out and enjoy company of the child.
3. Is quick to "catch the child being good."	3. Is quick to "catch the child being bad."
4. Sensitive to the child's needs and viewpoints.	4. Isn't sensitive to the child's needs and viewpoints.
Take Charge	**Unduly Permissive**
1. Clearly states rules or the consequences for violations.	1. Doesn't clearly state rules, consequences for violations.
2. Firmly or consistently enforces rules.	2. Doesn't firmly or consistently enforce rules.
3. Rarely gives in to child's unreasonable demands.	3. Is likely to give in to child's unreasonable demands.

❤

CHAPTER TWO

LEADERSHIP STYLES

Being a parent puts you in an official position. You're an authority and an expert with considerable power over the life of your child or children. You're a leader, and whether you realize it or not, you lead your children every day. If you don't lead directly, you still influence your children by being in their presence.

Children imitate their caregivers. A major part of your job is to show your children acceptable, logical, and respectful ways of thinking and behaving.

When your children are very young, your leadership role is relentless (remember your "Employment Opportunity"). Whether you feel up to it or not, you're in charge. You are the one who sets the rules and routines. And it's up to you to make sure that your children understand them. You can't avoid making daily decisions about how to discipline.

To be an effective leader, you need to make a plan—like the one Pat made with Chelsea to improve her grades—and follow through so the rules are obeyed and the job gets done.

Four Ways to Lead

Each of the four leadership styles (as shown in the chart on the following page) is useful, depending on *the specific needs of the situation*. Most parents use all four styles daily.

PARENTS
have a
CHOICE ✓
as to which
LEADERSHIP STYLE
to use.

 TAKE CHARGE (Directive)

 BENEVOLENT (Kindness)

 DEMOCRATIC (Negotiate)

 HANDS OFF (Freedom)

Taking Charge

Many times the simplest and best leadership style is to take charge, be a director. The parent is using his or her authority to provide firm direction, structure, and training.

Here's an example. Jennifer (5) and Jason (3) quarrel. Jason throws a toy at Jennifer and Jennifer hits Jason hard. Maxine, their mother, says, "Jennifer and Jason, you're not to hit or hurt each other. Play time is over for now. Both of you find something to do where you can leave each other alone." Maxine stands there until both children are occupied in different play activities. Maxine was consistent and firm. She gave reasons, set limits, and followed through. She was a disciplinarian. That's what "taking charge" is all about.

Benevolent

Skillful parents always cultivate a benevolent style with their children (and not a malevolent one). Their approach combines kindness, nurturing, and acceptance. They have compassion and they encourage parent-child bonding. The benevolent parent is a peacemaker. While this may be a parent's overriding method, there are some times that call for a little extra kindness. If Maxine, in her resolution to the toy fight, were to choose this role, she might handle Jennifer and Jason's problem in the following way.

"Jennifer and Jason, we're going to have a snack and go to the park where you'll have more space to play. Let's ask your friends if they can come along."

Maxine wants to keep harmony, and decides how to solve the problem without addressing the problem directly. The benevolent parent empathizes with the children's point of view and maintains harmony by helping children feel good about themselves and others.

Democratic

This style relies on the use of participation in decision making. A parent negotiates through problems by encouraging children to express their points of view. You encourage a child to listen receptively to the other child's point of view, and to yours as well. You allow children to "experiment" with what they believe are good ideas. This method of parenting allows experience to be the teacher, and it fosters independent thinking and confidence. Here's how Maxine could have used a democratic leadership style.

"Jennifer and Jason, please sit down," says Maxine. "You seem to be having some problems getting along. Jennifer, what do you think needs to be done?"

Jennifer says, "Jason should play in his room."

Jason says, "Jennifer should go play in her room and leave me alone."

Maxine responds with, "Do you agree that playing in separate places is a good idea for now?"

They both solemnly nod "Yes."

"Okay, good. I like the way you can solve problems." Both of the children leave to find something else to do.

The democratic parent says, "My job is to guide children so they can learn to solve their own problems."

Hands-off

This style is non-directive. Children are encouraged to assume as much responsibility as they can handle. The goal is to allow them the freedom to experiment and to learn from their experience on their own terms. The parent is accessible to provide direction, if necessary. Let's see Maxine in action as a hands-off leader.

Maxine thinks, "Oh, well, another case of sibling rivalry. They'll work it out themselves. I won't interfere." She keeps a sharp eye on them to make sure they don't hurt each other. Eventually, they solve their own problem and find another activity. The hands-off parent says, "If I don't interfere, the children will work it out by themselves."

Children often think of better solutions than we can. When we give attention to squabbles, it can perpetuate them. The hands-off method can build good thinking skills because children left to their own resources must decide how to solve their own problems. Be careful, though, not to resort to hands-off parenting just because you're too tired to assume a stronger leadership role. Sometimes children aren't able to make wise choices on their own. Too much of the hands-off style is overly permissive, leaving children in charge and without parental guidance.

Deciding Which Style to Use

Which leadership style should you use and when? When do you need to move in and take charge? When is it best to move away and keep hands-off? There are no easy answers, but here's a parenting success secret—you must consider *the needs of the situation,* and decide accordingly which leadership style will work best with your children. It's important that you use all four parenting leadership styles frequently. In any given exchange with a child, you may be taking charge, pulling back into hands-off, shifting into democratic negotiating, and end with a benevolent pat on the back. I'd like to see parents use these styles more deliberately. Don't just pick one style and routinely use it; develop the breadth to dance with them all!

Fred's story, told to us during a Parent Connection session, illustrates how to use the four leadership styles. Fred is a gentle, sensitive man who takes his fathering duties seriously. He speaks in a low-pitched monotone, and he's as predictable as an old stone.

For the last five years, Fred has had the sole physical custody of his daughters. Their mother, who lives in the same town, never enjoyed being a parent. While she became more impatient and critical with the children, he bent over backward to be patient. Eventually they separated.

He's not sure what to say to his sixteen-year-old daughter, Nicki, when she arrives at the bus station the next morning. Two weeks previously, she left him a note that said, "I'll be home in a few. Nicki." *Four days later* she called her father from Oklahoma. She and her friend, Pam, had accepted a ride from an acquaintance who was driving to New York:

"Will you drop us at Pam's relatives?"

"Sure. Come on." And off they went.

"Dad, will you send me a plane ticket home?" Nicki asked. Fred wired a bus ticket instead, expecting her to jump on the next bus. He wanted her to study for the high school proficiency exam, which was coming up soon. But she delayed her return even further, until she had been gone for a total of two weeks.

Nicki would arrive home only twenty-four hours before the exam. Furthermore, Nicki's Aunt Sara had called that day to say that Nicki had changed a check she gave her from $16.49 to $46.49. And, of course, there was the whole issue of the reckless cross-country adventure.

Fred went on to tell us that the month before, Nicki had left for three weeks to live with a carpenter who was 21. He had lots of money, but lots of demands, too. Nicki thought he was a drag and moved back with her dad. She was not going to school. He didn't know if she had a drug history or if she was sexually active, although he had suspicions. Nicki is power drunk, totally in control of her father, and Fred is playing the naive victim.

I had Fred role-play his bus stop meeting with Nicki. He gazed at another student with big brooding eyes, sighed, and said, "Are you okay? Well, I guess you just got fed up and felt like a vacation. Are you glad to be back home? I want you to know that I really love you and that I accept you as you are. If there is anything you want to talk about, I'm willing to listen." That's the *benevolent* style in action.

Fred had the right receptive listening technique, but the wrong timing. He had lost all control over his daughter. He wasn't about to get it back with the soft touch. The needs of the situation called for a firmer approach. He played the part of Nicki and I played him.

When she got off the bus, I said, "Hi. Any luggage?"

"No."

"The car's over here." Silence. That's *hands-off*.

Once we were in the car, I said, "Nicki, this behavior is wrong, wrong,

wrong. You've been away for two weeks without permission. What you're doing is out of control. [He threw me an attitude look, and then I really got into my part of being Dad.] You have no right to take advantage of the privileges you've been given. Running away instead of solving your problems is selfish and dangerous. This behavior has got to stop *now*. Your aunt said that the check she gave you for $16.49 came back to her for $46.49. That's forgery. [Fred pretended to cry.] You can cry all you want. I'm not impressed. You can turn on and off tears like a water faucet. Crying isn't going to fix this problem. You're in pretty deep." This is the *take charge* mode working.

We stopped the role-play while I coached Fred. He said, "I've never talked to her like that! I think you ought to be compassionate and understanding." I do, too—but there's a time and a place for that. Fred's situation is urgent. He needs to take charge—to be assertive by being direct and firm, get his ideas across by speaking from the gut. It was time to rely on facts to express himself. I advised him to avoid starting his talk with disempowering questions such as: Are you okay? Why did you do it? Don't you think staying away for two weeks is wrong? One of the most important secrets of parenting success is using statement sentences with your children rather than asking them questions. I recommend saying specifically what you think and what you want. The direct approach of a statement sentence works wonders. Once you've mastered this technique, you'll have a *breakthrough* as an effective communicator. Read again how I handled the role-play with Fred. "Any luggage?" is the only question you'll find.

I also advised Fred to offer Nicki a choice of staying or leaving his home. If she decides to stay, she must obey his rules; if she decides to go, he'll work with her to find an appropriate place to stay. I also told him to file an "incorrigible report" at the police department for her.

We went back to role-playing. I said, "Nicki, you'll no longer take advantage of the home I've provided for you. You have to decide first if you're willing to live here and live by the rules, or if we're to find another place for you. Three choices that come to mind are your mother, juvenile hall, or a boarding school. I've gone to the police station and filed an incorrigible child report. If you leave home again, falsify a check, or do anything else that I've taught you is seriously wrong, I'm going to press legal charges against you. You're *never* to leave a note saying 'I'll be home in a few' and not let me know where you're going. From now on, don't you even think about changing the amount on a check. That's fraud. You're to earn the $30 you owe Aunt Sara and pay her by this time next week."

I continued playing the "new Fred." "If you choose to stay, I want your understanding of this living arrangement in writing by 6:00 P.M. Sunday evening. After I look it over, we'll discuss it." This makes the shift to *democratic* leadership.

"If you're taking the high school proficiency exam tomorrow, arrange a way to wake up on time and find transportation to get there." The *hands-off* approach.

Fred's situation is so urgent that he has to shift his approach dramatically. Being the benevolent leader isn't working. As a take-charge leader, he offers his daughter choices. He put her in a position of negotiating her living situation. He's become a firm disciplinarian. He's no longer fueling her intoxication with power.

Fred seemed to get it, all but the hands-off part of not waking her up and driving her to the proficiency exam. "Why shouldn't I do that?"

I responded that she isn't interested in the high school proficiency exam as much as he is. It's another source of power struggle and it isn't urgent. She can take the exam at another time. He needs to stop being a "soft touch" and let her experience the consequences of her choices, starting *right now*. Getting Nicki under control is an emergency situation. She's at high risk for being seduced, raped, pregnant, acquiring AIDS, getting hooked on drugs, turning into a prostitute, or falling prey to a host of flim-flam artists who know how to tame rebellious teenagers.

Does this mean that whenever runaways come home they should get the same kind of treatment? Absolutely not! This isn't a formula for how to treat runaways. The leadership style you use depends on the needs of the situation, and other situations may be different. Fred is too soft, too polite. He uses only one leadership style—benevolent—and it isn't working. He has only a piece of the whole parenting picture. To know what you can do in a runaway child situation, you have to figure out what the child is running from, what the child is running to, and why. What is the child's point of view? Some parents are so rigid that they need to use more democracy and benevolence in their leadership role. However, tender loving care doesn't always mean being "sweet."

You will have unlocked a major secret to parenting success when you understand these leadership styles. When a child is likely to be hurt, you need to move in and take charge. When you believe your children can figure out the solution to their own problems, you need to step back. It's your job to influence and control your children's behavior by using teaching methods other than pain. Your leadership skills can provide your children with a solid foundation on which they will build their lives. And every day your parenting example matters.

If You Have a Gift to Give

After hearing stories from thousands of parents about how miserable family life is for them, I've discovered one fundamental truth, one which parents usually don't want to hear—children are often blamed for the parent's problems. Blaming a child has the effect of removing responsibility from the parent to figure out better ways of handling problem situations. A more appropriate response for many parents is, "It's really my problem. It's not the child's fault that I'm uncomfortable."

An extraordinary father once said to me, "If I have a gift to give, I have a responsibility to give it in a way that it can be received." He influenced me to package my insights, knowledge, and skills in a way that I can effectively get this sensitive issue across to parents. Knowledge is not innate; we all acquire knowledge from someone else. At The Parent Connection, I package my gift with understanding, hope and optimism, and then I go to work on the parents.

Many parents come to The Parent Connection thinking that their children are 100% of the family's problems, but I know better. Court-referred parents (parents who are told that they have to take a parenting class by an officer of the court) often ask me, "Why am I being punished? I didn't commit the crime." This sentiment reflects the view that the parent education they're required to take at The Parent Connection is punishment for something they aren't guilty of to begin with.

Try this little exercise. Point your finger at someone or something right now. Study your hand. How many fingers point back at you? Three? The forefinger represents blame. In The Blame Game, if something is wrong, it's someone else's fault. The three fingers pointing back at you are The Denial Game. That's the game of "Not me!" Many people are in serious denial over their own participation in existing family problems. Blaming everyone else for what happens is an easy trap to fall into. The idea is for parents not to place blame, but to accept the responsibility for solving the problems. Accepting this responsibility may be scary at first.

The Millionaire Who Almost Walked Away

Don called for an appointment to see me at The Parent Connection.

He talked very fast, but there were many disruptions and I was placed on hold several times. "My ex-wife wants to destroy me. She used my money to buy a mansion and she lives there with her new husband. He's no good. They want to break me. Katie [his four-year-old daughter] loves me. She should be with me. They're trying to kill me. Now I can't see my daughter. I'm a good father. I give her horseback riding lessons. We have fun together. Is that bad? Now I can only see Katie if there's a monitor present. They hate me. They want to destroy me. Do you think I'm a bad parent?"

I suggested that he come in for a meeting so we could talk about what was going on. Don's thinking was scattered and paranoid. He was a wild man, living on an emotional roller coaster. He had made millions in real estate and other investments. He found himself in big trouble, however, when he told an investigating social worker, "I'm too busy to talk to you. Call my lawyer." His lawyer was out of town for two weeks. Don suddenly found out that social workers have power. He was slapped with monitored visits of two hours a week with his beautiful daughter, Katie.

For three months, while his business deteriorated, he became obsessed with the idea that his ex-wife was trying to destroy him. Taking most of my parenting classes privately, he was a fast learner. Once he gained an insight, he would explain several examples of how it could be used in actual parenting situations. He eventually tried the knowledge on for size with Katie in his two-hour weekend visits.

I believe that Don is an eccentric genius. I unsuccessfully tried to change his negative visualization about being destroyed, broken, and bankrupt. I continued to think, What can I do to reach this man? One day as Don was repeating his gloomy list and embellishing on how his ex-wife and her husband were so vicious and evil to him, I tried a new strategy.

I said, "Don, what have you done or said that has caused all this misery to happen to you?"

He immediately reacted, "Nothing. They're trying to destroy me."

"Why?"

"Because they want Katie all to themselves."

"Are they afraid of you?"

"No. They're crazy."

"Don, what are you doing or saying that is contributing to the problem?" I repeated.

"It isn't me. You don't believe me. They're trying to destroy me, make me go bankrupt, and lose all of my money." He became very agitated and he stood up and announced, "I don't have to stay here. I'm leaving."

He threw his workbook into his briefcase and snapped it shut. As he started toward the door, I held my breath. I was afraid that I'd gone too far, but he paused and grabbed the phone. He called his lawyer, who wasn't in. Then he called his father.

"Dad, tell her that it isn't my fault. She thinks it's my fault."

I spoke with his father at length. Don's father clearly didn't want to make things worse, and while he had some opinions, he didn't have much insight into what had gone so seriously wrong between Don and his ex-wife, Andrea.

I was relentless with Don, and in his next visits I continued to point out that we attract what we project. "Don, what have you done or said that has attracted this misery to you?" He wasn't used to having anyone stand up to him. He finally got to the point of admitting that he didn't know why they seemed to be picking on him. He finished the classes and signed up for more, but I didn't see him for several weeks.

He later called me to say, "Thank you, Jayne. You were the best thing that happened to me. Andrea saved my life. She doesn't hate me; she really loves me. I've seen a psychiatrist. I have a compulsive mental disorder and I'm on medication. I'm going to play it her way for a while."

Last week was Don's court date. He had stabilized his emotions and overall behavior and his full visitation rights were restored. He was back to "making deals," earning money, and continuing Katie's horseback riding lessons. Don's turning point was when he realized that maybe, just maybe, he was a part of the overall family problem. I helped make it safe for him to turn inward and take a good look at what was there.

Don's story helps illustrate one of the major secrets to parenting success—the way to transform children is to transform parents. The inescapable fact is that parents have the greater responsibility (from their greater experience, skills, and knowledge) for what happens in the family. They're the logical leaders. Showing you a better way to do your parenting job will automatically help your children.

❤

CHAPTER THREE

SELF-SACRIFICE IS NOT A VIRTUE

Parents must, of course, make sacrifices. You give up some time, money, energy, and resources when you parent—this is part of your job description. Children would not survive without a parent's care. And to be blunt, they need you more than you need them. While you can supply your own necessities, a child cannot. Does that mean that your children are more important than you? I don't think so. *Every family member is important.*

The key to successful parenting is to nurture yourself. Yes, that's right! Being a good parent doesn't rule out that you can be happy and take care of yourself. In fact, I'm going to tell you how your children are being harmed when you neglect your basic needs. Nurturing means providing yourself nourishment, support, and encouragement. It entails fostering good habits and acquiring knowledge. It also requires being able to think straight, loving yourself, and having the confidence to take care of yourself. You have to provide for your essential needs, build on your strengths, and minimize your weaknesses. You're in charge of treating yourself with sensitivity, and by being good to yourself, you'll be a better parent.

Being a good role model to your children takes time, practice, and know-how. Most of all, you must realize that taking care of *you* is one of the most important things you must do every day. Maintaining balance in your life—both physically and mentally—is the greatest gift you can give your child. Your child will admire you and want to be strong like you. Now *there's* a parenting secret worth knowing.

Self-esteem is the way we bond with the "self." Bonding means having a strong and enduring quality of affection for "who I am." It's a friendship that reflects an attitude of "I like me, I'm here for me, I'm safe with me; the relationship I have with myself has integrity, reliability, and consistency."

Punishing and Spoiling Your Children

When I began The Parent Connection, I didn't expect to be working with parents who severely punish their children. Here are examples of these challenging parents:

- Quiet, sweet Leslie exploded one night and used an extension cord to beat her son who had taken money out of her grandma's purse.
- Gloria talked non-stop about what a dirty, low-life, stupid son she had. "He's just like his father."
- Bonnie put her young daughter's hand in a fire to teach her not to touch fire.

I've heard people say that such parents don't love their children, but I haven't met a single parent lacking in love. Leslie, Gloria, and Bonnie do love their children. Not one of them, however, knows how to do a better job. Leslie doesn't know how to manage her anger. Gloria doesn't know about the need to protect her son's self-esteem. Bonnie didn't understand how to teach her daughter about fire or other dangers.

The "lacking in love" argument is too simple. I decided to call the classes at The Parent Connection "Skillful Parenting: Because Love is Not Enough." If love were enough, parents wouldn't face all of these problems. I don't believe that parents abuse or neglect their children on purpose. It isn't deliberate.

Which leads me to another parenting secret—parents neglect and abuse their children because they neglect and abuse themselves. They don't know a better way to manage their own lives. When parents aren't taking care of their own basic needs, their children present them with more deprivation and stress than they know how to handle. Something snaps.

Moving Beyond Self-Sacrifice

Many parents believe that once you have children, you're obligated to sacrifice your own welfare for their sakes. They incorrectly assume that they aren't as important as their children and that a parent's role is the constant surrendering of their own good. "Children come first," many of us grew up hearing. This results in parents who are continuously off-balance. Resentments build up and there is a loss of their own importance in the family structure.

One common denominator in most of the poorly functioning families I've seen is parents who are self-sacrificing. This, too, is a form of abuse and neglect, and I've seen parents and family experts overlook the importance of stopping parental self-sacrifice as a way of healing the family. When parents neglect themselves, their children inevitably become victims. Parents whose own needs are neglected are not functioning at their best and often are in no condition to take care of their children. Frustrated parents can harm children on many levels, and that's certainly not living up to the parent's job of being a positive primary role model.

Pat is an example of a self-sacrificing parent. Working hard selling real estate and raising two children at the same time, she provides all the basics for her children. She's exhausted, however, and has no time to rest and recover her energy. Her children demand to have their way when they're around Pat. She gives in to their whims because she thinks that it's her duty. She doesn't feel appreciated. Her resentments build.

The self-sacrificing parent thinks, "Other people are more important than I am," then resents being taken advantage of.

Gerry, my earlier example of the parent who dreaded going home from work, saw immediately where he was self-sacrificing. "I want quiet time with my wife. I want to enjoy my kids and not be so busy that I can't have fun with them." They had the means to hire Natalie, a high school student who loves children, to help out around the house three times a week. Natalie became part of the parent team. She enjoyed having a "babysitting job" while the parents were around. Many times she prepared dinner while Gerry consulted with Sandra about her homework and attended to bathtime and storytelling. Natalie became Maxine and Gerry's right arm. When she graduated and left for college, she trained one of her good friends to take over. This arrangement was not as expensive as a full-time housekeeper or nanny, and it was well worth the expense to have an extra hand during the important evening hours.

Needs are different from wants, luxuries, or desires. You *need* sleep, good food, time to relax or pursue hobbies and exercise, and medical care when you're ill. When you neglect these, you can become run down, sick, or burned out. The end result can be the inability for you to think or act wisely.

Your children constantly have needs, but so do you! What a juggling match it is, too. Young children want and require attention now. They have very little understanding or tolerance for delays.

Does this scene sound familiar? Maxine, the mom, is coming down with a cold. "I want a cookie. I want a cookie!" Jason (3) whines. "You'll have to wait until after dinner for a snack so you won't spoil your appetite," Maxine asserts. "I want a cookie now!" Jason shrieks. Maxine thinks, This is such a little thing, but I'm in no mood for this.

Should Maxine give Jason a cookie now and buy a little peace? Or should she stand firm? The appropriate answer brings me to another parenting secret—there's a fine line between healthy sacrifice and unhealthy sacrifice; healthy sacrifices are what's reasonable and fair in any situation. Maxine might say, "Jason, I don't feel well. I need quiet. If you want a cookie, you'll have to wait until after dinner. We're eating in fifteen minutes. You'll have to wait."

Maxine sets limits for Jason and shows that she's sensitive to her son's wishes. She gives him a reasonable time frame when his wish will be fulfilled. She tells him that she has a need, too (hers is for quiet). Finally, she expresses herself firmly by setting a limit: "You may have a cookie after dinner."

Discussions about child abuse and neglect are common, but what about *parent* abuse and neglect? Children who are abusive of their parents have not been taught to behave with regard and respect for others' needs. Parents have rights, too, and you have an obligation to stand up for your rights! "Yes," you might say, "but the problem is getting my children to cooperate." My reply is with another parenting secret—with instruction and consistency from parents, youngsters learn that other people have needs. Your children learn because you tell them and then follow through to see that your needs are met. These lessons teach children that there are good reasons why they have to wait. It's sometimes more important that Mom or Dad take care of their needs than to grant the child's wish, all depending on what's reasonable and fair in the situation.

Learn to distinguish between sacrifice that's part of the job of parenting and self-sacrifice that's excessive and harmful. If you wear out your body, where will you live? If you lose your mind, how will you think? Who will take care of your children if you are unable to do so? Why does it take a crisis before so many parents understand the necessity of taking care of "me"? You, as the parent, have a primary responsibility to attend to your own needs.

Weakness Attracts Weakness

Sacrifices which undermine your physical or mental well-being keep you from performing at your best and make you a less effective parent. If you have low energy, are in pain or feel run down, then you're in physical jeopardy. Or if you're fearful, nervous, depressed or frustrated, you're not mentally healthy and aren't a good role model for your children. Unless you want your children to deprive themselves of life's necessities, then don't deprive yourself. Remember Pat and her "two stubborn brats"? As soon as she saw a way to fill her needs and reach her potential, her children became cooperative. When she learned how to live harmoniously, so did they.

You owe it to yourself and to all of those you love to take good care of *you*. If you're presently not able to get enough rest, good food, exercise, peace and quiet, hobbies, entertainment and regular medical care, then you have some serious problems to solve. Take time now to start working on them. Figure out whether you're being self-sacrificing in an unhealthy way.

❤

CHAPTER FOUR

R=TLC
A FORMULA TO
PULL IT ALL TOGETHER

Do you want your children to grow up to be responsible? After asking thousands of parents this question, I have never heard anyone say "No." If raising our children to be responsible adults is every parent's goal, then why do so many children grow up to lie, cheat, steal, and act cruelly? This formula helps explain what goes wrong, and how to steer children right.

What does "being responsible" mean? One definition is "the ability to respond appropriately." The "R" in our formula R=TLC stands for *being responsible*. This formula has Tender Loving Care or TLC built into it as a reminder that everyone has needs to be taken care of—even you.

Each person acts according to what he or she understands to be right or appropriate. The concept of responsibility can be slippery because it differs from one person to the next. What we believe is responsible often reflects the culture in which we were raised.

The Johnsons, for instance, are well-educated. They want their children to like school, to go to good universities, and to practice white collar professions. That's their vision of "responsibility" for their children.

The parent in the Smith family firmly believes that no one should try to be better than anyone else. Everyone shows responsibility by working hard and by working together.

The Garcia family is headed by parents who want their children to be provided with sound religious education. This includes paying for private schooling at their church.

The meaning of "responsible" depends on cultural and personal beliefs and values. However, here's a parenting secret you'll always want to keep in mind—no one can be responsible unless he or she has developed three essential qualities of character: good thinking, loving, and confidence.

Thinking

In our formula R=TLC the "T" stands for *thinking*. The more you strengthen your ability to reason and to solve problems, the better you function. Intelligence is more than what you inherit, it is developed mostly by what you learn. There are many ways to learn, some having nothing to do with school. Attentive parents routinely teach children to be rational and to show common sense in all situations.

Gerry, our hard-working father example, could see that Jason (3) was developing an aggressive streak. When other children got in his way, he shoved them. He wouldn't make any allowances for sharing. In class I suggested that they get a family dog and that Jason learn to take care of it. Many children learn how to treat others by transferring their affection for a pet to people. Gerry and Maxine took their three children to an animal shelter where they picked out a dog. The puppy, Gypsy, was great fun for a while, but one day Gerry reported to the class that he had observed Jason getting mad and yanking Gypsy's tail roughly enough to make her yelp.

We role-played an appropriate response. "Playing rough and bullying Gypsy could hurt her, Jason. Puppies' tails weren't meant to be pulled. You wouldn't like to be treated like that, would you? Puppies like to have fun. Let's play with Gypsy together." The technique he used was to teach right from wrong, set limits, and follow through. He also added The Golden Rule—"You wouldn't like to be treated that way, would you?"

No school teacher or peer will ever have as much influence over your child as you, the parent and primary role model. If you demonstrate good thinking in the way you solve problems, your children will learn to solve problems successfully.

Next week Gerry reported his progress to the class. He and Jason had a delightful time playing chase with Gypsy. Later he showed Jason where the clean dog dishes were kept and how to measure out the right amount of food. He let Jason take charge of feeding her. Gerry was generous in catching Jason being good to his pet. He pointed out what was right about his behavior. Jason was treating Gypsy with TLC, the same method Gerry was using on his son.

Gerry taught Jason simple facts about puppy tails, proper play, and a puppy's need for food and being happy. He modeled the right behavior and encouraged Jason to do the same. This underscores another parenting secret of great value—successful parents supply their children with examples to help them understand. They teach children the difference between reality and fantasy, between facts and opinions. They continually encourage children to seek what is true and to take appropriate action.

Remember Wanda, the mother who had serious trouble with her knife-wielding daughter? Wanda's younger daughter, Sherryl, stubbornly refuses to accept her share of the household chores. She complains, "Tanika didn't have to help. Why should I be your slave?" It was true that Tanika (the knife-wielding teen) didn't help. Wanda didn't want another daughter in juvenile hall. She told Sherryl, "Yes, it's true that Tanika got by without doing her share of the chores. You can see where that got her. You're not Tanika. It's only fair that everyone in the family accepts their share of the chores and helps out. You're to make a plan, then tell me what chores you're willing to do and when is the best time for them to be done."

Sherryl's plan showed a minimal effort. Wanda acknowledged her for her willingness to help and then said, "I think it would be more fair if you included dusting and vacuuming once a week. You can decide when is the best time, but I need to know your choice so this isn't something we're going to fight over." Sherryl picked Saturday mornings.

Wanda was also learning another secret from our parenting class—the "Catch Them Being Good" technique. Reward the many good things you find your children doing. It will perpetuate good behavior. After Sherryl complied and made a plan, Wanda offered her daughter some incentives when chores were done on Saturday as planned. Together they chose activities that were fun for both of them, such as going to the movies and shopping.

Wanda was determined that her daughter Sherryl wouldn't walk in Tanika's footsteps. This time, using her power as a parent with a democratic leadership style, she didn't lose control of the situation. She began teaching Sherryl to be fair and to think of other people's rights and feelings. Every day parents have countless opportunities to show their children how to be good thinkers. It begins when adults start thinking positively about their job as parents.

Loving

"L" in the R=TLC formula stands for *loving*. The critical first stage of helping children develop into loving people is to encourage them to love themselves.

Memorize this parenting secret—it's only from a foundation of self-love that children mature to become loving toward others. It's a terrible mistake to associate self-love with being selfish, bad, or spoiled. A healthy narcissism is essential to expanding one's feelings of love toward others. From self-love, children learn to please others, to be fair, and to respect the law. During this natural progression, children learn to be ethical and caring individuals. Considerable Tender Loving Care (TLC) is the best way to teach children how to love and to think. The most successful parents love themselves and assure that their children's needs are met regularly. Their positive self-esteem and self-love rubs off on their children.

Jason learned about love by mastering how to care for his dog, Gypsy. His father, Gerry, continued to encourage Jason's caring behavior by acknowledging his successes, and remembering to "catch him being good." Jason now views himself as worthwhile and extends this good feeling to his pet. It could have been otherwise, however. If Jason hadn't been taught a better way to have fun, he could have ended up thinking that hurting animals is fun.

Confidence

"C" stands for *confidence* in the R=TLC formula. Confidence means the courage to take action: to stand up for one's self and to make independent decisions. Just being a good thinker and a loving person doesn't make you a responsible person. You need the courage of your convictions to speak up and to act on what you believe is right. This requires confidence.

Gerry called me to talk about an incident in school that was directly related to what had happened when Jason was three. In first grade Jason had encountered two bullies on the playground who pushed him around and called him a sissy. Jason knew that he didn't deserve to be treated this way any more than Gypsy did. His father had taught him not to be a bully. He told his father about the playground incident. Gerry went with him to the teacher and asked that the offending boys be taught to behave more sensitively. Jason no longer played the role of a bully himself and he had the confidence to stand up for himself. He was also backed up by good parental support.

When Tanika and her mother, Wanda, were reunited after Tanika's baby was born, there were many opportunities for Wanda to demonstrate confidence. Tanika was pleasantly surprised at her mother's sensitivity and willingness to help. Wanda didn't realize that when she learned how to be more confident about her parenting skills, she would be passing this knowledge on to a new generation. Tanika began to mirror her mother's self-esteem and become more confident in her parenting abilities. It wasn't long before they could laugh and joke about that frightening night when Tanika threatened her mother's life.

R=TLC: Your Formula for the Good Life

Society has changed dramatically from when you were a child. We can't begin to anticipate what our children will face in their lifetimes. How can you prepare them for an uncertain future?

The best way is to teach children the meaning of responsibility so that they'll be able to decide on appropriate responses to different situations. Children need to learn good thinking skills, to form strategies for positive action, and to understand the difference between fact and fiction. They need to establish good values. This also entails liking themselves and having self-esteem so they can love other people and the planet we live on. That's the Good Life for one and all.

We should never forget that children learn not only by what we tell them but by how they see us conduct our lives. By showing our approval when they act constructively, we can create an atmosphere where they can build their confidence.

Our formula R=TLC is a universal formula for the Good Life. It embodies both a *goal* and a *method*. The common goal is for children to grow up to be responsible, mature adults. The best method is consistent with Tender Loving Care. When parents are positive leaders, they demonstrate good thinking, loving and confidence, and by doing this, they optimize their chances for parenting success.

The Good Life awaits you once you embrace the R=TLC formula and shed the burden of self-sacrifice. But there's still another barrier to parental success left to tackle—misguided love—and we'll turn to that issue in the next chapter.

♥

CHAPTER FIVE

MISGUIDED LOVE

We've been examining key ideas about the parents' role, leadership styles, and healthy vs. unhealthy sacrifices. I shared with you The Parent Connection's formula, R=TLC, for building great relationships with your children. Now I'd like to turn your attention to irresponsible parenting. Almost always, parents try to justify this kind of behavior as an expression of love for their children. However, this method of "loving children" invariably causes more harm than good. Let's look at the many faces of irresponsibility by seeing how misguided a parent's love can be.

The Boss: Sit Down and Shut Up, Because I Said So

The *authoritarian* style of leadership has been around for a long time. While some authoritarian parents rule from the top down and are not cruel, others follow a darker way of raising children. The "sit down, shut up, and do as I say" school of thought is a serious concern. Children are to be seen and not heard. They dare not speak their opinions or get in the way of adults. In short, children are treated as puppets, pawns or non-persons, not as individuals with feelings and rights.

Authoritarians, when found in government positions, are called autocrats. Autocrats aren't interested in debates and will not tolerate disagreement with their views. They must have obedience from their followers to stay in power, and they don't consider the best interests of others. Because they don't want competition, encouraging competent people to lead isn't part of their formula for success. They're oppressors, not liberators.

Some authoritarian parents don't understand about building self-esteem or empowering children with their inherent goodness and self-worth. They aren't concerned with helping children grow to their maximum potential. Like autocrats, they motivate by fear. They spell out how awful the consequences or punishment would be for disobedience. They inspire in children a fear of doing nothing other than obeying. But when confronted with their behavior, they'll insist their actions are based on love for their children (albeit a warped and misguided sense of love that ignores the negative consequences to their children).

Individuals who grew up under this system of child rearing cringe at the abuses they've experienced. They remember the beatings, going to bed without dinner, standing in the corner for hours, and being terrified of how much worse it could get. Sometimes, they even feared for their survival.

Just as misguided, psychological abuse doesn't leave scars that you can easily see. "You stupid idiot!" "You're worthless!" "You've ruined my life!" "I wish that you'd never been born!" Words like these can hit as hard as a fist.

Emotional deprivation follows from such sentiments. There's no affection, no expression of enduring love and no encouragement to greater success, so children are cut off at the earliest, most critical stage of love they need. They live a survival existence. Authoritarian abuse has often resulted in the arrested development of children.

He'll Be a Star

One day a social worker called and said, "Jayne, I'm sending you a special case named Jessie. See if you can get him to loosen up. He rules his child with a vice-like grip." When Jessie walked into class, he was ramrod straight with a look of "There isn't anything you can tell me that I don't know already." When it was his turn to describe his family situation, he claimed there were no problems other than a pesky social worker he needed to get off his back and a kid who didn't try hard enough.

Jessie's son, Willie (11), signed up for Little League at his father's insistence. Willie was looking forward to playing, but now he's miserable. Jessie constantly corrects him. Although Willie is only an average player, Jessie wants him to be the star Jessie wasn't when he was a child. Jessie is reliving his baseball days through Willie, and doesn't allow his son to find his own way or make his own mistakes.

Jessie is a boss. He's rigid and afraid of losing control. He's intolerant of mistakes. He snaps, "You should have known that." Or, "I told you that already."

You can hear bosses barking commands. "Put that down." "Stop that." "Be quiet." This is their favorite form of communication. Bosses impose unrealistic standards on their children because they don't understand the normal stages of child development. They certainly don't understand how to protect a child's self-esteem and build confidence. They want children to act and think like miniature adults, and when children act like children, "the boss" is quick to criticize. This is misguided love.

Stop Spoiling Now

What does *spoiling* mean? My dictionary says:

1. To damage or harm one's excellence, value, or usefulness.
2. To impair one's character by excessively indulgent treatment.

Sometimes the way parents use words, bad means good and good means bad. "Look at Sara. She's such a princess, she's spoiled rotten." Her parents mean that they're proud of treating her well. Bad means good. When parents take their children to special events, give them money when it's needed and in general treat them with abundance, it doesn't mean that they're "spoiling" them.

Prosperity and abundance are part of the Good Life. Children deserve to be treated well, and it isn't spoiling to do so. For most of us, giving is more gratifying than receiving. It feels good. I don't believe that many of the people who say that they're spoiling their children are actually doing damage or harm to their children's excellence, value, or usefulness. They're not impairing their children's character so that they'll grow up to be sociopaths, people with no moral conscience, who only know how to take and how to abuse people in the process.

Then what *is* spoiling? Spoiling is letting children watch TV for seven hours a day—the current U. S. national average. This means that they aren't exercising, socializing, reading, helping around the house, and a host of other activities that build character, strengthen the body, and encourage responsible development.

Spoiling is indulging children with material things. Some parents try to buy their children's love with an excessive number of toys, a personal

TV, and expensive clothes. Nothing's too good for my child! Parents may be inadvertently warping their children's inner development into thinking that material possessions and status is the Good Life.

Spoiling is letting children eat junk food. A recent statistic points out that only one in four children eat the recommended daily amounts of fruits and vegetables. Many parents don't insist that their children eat fruits and vegetables because they were raised in a time when their importance wasn't understood. Spoiling is letting children decide their own routines, like when to go to bed, when to eat, or whether to do homework. Spoiling is not insisting that a child clean up after himself or herself. Spoilers are parents who've fallen into the trap of letting children do whatever they want whenever they want because they're afraid that their children won't like them if they say No.

We aren't spoiling children when we discipline them by teaching right from wrong, setting limits, and following through to see that they've learned their lessons by behaving appropriately. Spoiling children means to neglect to train children in responsible behavior. Spoiling is neglect. It's misguided love.

The Buddy: Give Them What They Want

Some parents hate authoritarian methods so much they go to the opposite extreme, *permissiveness*. It's another form of misguided love. "Whatever you want, honey." The practice of "give them what they want" can lead to disaster. These parents don't protect children from their own innocence.

Children think in terms of the immediate. They want what they want when they want it. They hate "No" and will get angry when they don't get their way. Babies throw tantrums because they don't have words to express themselves. They rely on body language and noise. When babies cry and shake their fists and kick, they get what they want: a bottle, a change, or a remedy for colic. Sometimes the tantrum habit survives long after children have learned better ways of expressing themselves.

During the "terrible twos," many parents continue to give in to temper tantrums rather than take the time to correct this behavior. Giving in only encourages children to use anger and emotion rather than words. A temper tantrum is no more than an exercise to express "I'm unhappy. I'm very young and I don't know a better way to express myself." It's your job to teach your child a better way of how to get personal needs met.

Here's a great parenting secret—deep down, children are less interested in getting their way than parents may assume; most children would rather have parents who provide them with what's in their best interest. Children aren't able to look at the big picture; that's the parents' job.

The Cupcake that Tasted Funny

Here's a Parent Connection example of permissiveness in action. Naomi described being raised by parents who rarely set limits and didn't understand the importance of healthful foods. They indulged her desires for cake, cookies, ice cream, chips, and sodas whenever she wanted them. Her parents said "okay" to sugary, fat-filled treats when she wasn't hungry for a good dinner. In her family they celebrated with food and consoled themselves with over-indulgence whenever problems arose. She confessed that later she put on eighty-one pounds in one year while she and her husband Art were having financial problems. Her inability to control her weight led to serious medical problems.

Naomi and Art are prime examples of *permissive* parents. They have a classic marriage where Art is the chief breadwinner and fixes things when he's at home. Naomi, the primary caregiver of their three children, serves on the board of The Parent Connection.

Naomi told me the story about how Danny (now 12) once brought home a chocolate cupcake from school. I asked, "What's so unusual about that?" She laughed and tried to explain.

When Naomi's children were little, she would routinely ask them, "What do you want to eat?" She made her shopping list from what the children said. The children usually made their selections from the commercials they saw on TV. It never crossed her mind to take charge of what they ate.

This was typical of her parenting style. The children were permitted to go to bed when they felt like it, they watched TV as much as they wanted, they did homework if they got around to it, and they rarely helped around the house.

Three years ago Naomi attended a Parent Connection lecture on family nutrition. I had drawn a simple grid of "healthful food/unhealthful food," and the parents helped me fill it in. After the class, she told Art, "We have to make some changes in the way we eat." Art had no complaint. He was permissive as well—"Whatever you want, honey."

As a result of the nutrition class, Naomi became more selective in buying food. She chose whole grain and fresh items that weren't loaded with salt, sugar, fat, or preservatives. Her children began to feel better and had fewer colds. Naomi was delighted to find that she was losing weight on their new diet.

She asked Danny what he thought of the cupcake he brought home from school. He said, "It had a *'funny* taste.'" He didn't finish it. He'd lost his taste for fatty, sugary foods.

We rapidly adapt to the taste of foods we're used to eating. We can train our taste buds to enjoy healthier foods. Most children will choose the sugary, salty, high fat, unhealthful foods. When we're very young, we think, What I want right now is most important. Young children don't understand the role of food in promoting growth and health, nor do they know that what they eat today may have consequences tomorrow and possibly years from now. Your responsibility as a parent is to be a leader in teaching children behavior that positively effects their overall health and well-being.

I Want My Children to Like Me

Overly-permissive parents see themselves as their children's buddy, as equals in authority and power. They don't take charge as leaders, and they don't set appropriate limits for their children. They say no, but aren't likely to stick to it or follow through. "Buddy parents" feel that what a child demands is what a child should have. They're fooled into thinking that a child really wants what he or she says.

Actually, children feel most secure when parents take charge and are firm on the important things. Remember the school teacher that you just loved because she wouldn't let you get by with a less-than-adequate job? We remember these people more than the ones who didn't hold us accountable. Children live in the moment without thinking of the consequences of things that aren't good for them. They look to their parents to provide guidance and set limits. Naomi didn't understand that children want their parents to take charge by being responsible people. Her family's quality of life improved when she became a better leader in her family.

A permissive parent's attitude is to *give children whatever they want.* Often they support this point of view with ideas such as "You're only a kid once" or "I just hate to say 'No'" or "I want my child to love me." Children already have the attitude of "I'm entitled to whatever I want when I want it. You don't have a right to say 'no' to me." This feels natural to a child, who expects immediate gratification. Children have to be trained to think maturely and respect their parents' guidance.

As I was about to begin a class section on permissive parenting, I got a call from a mother whose teenage daughter was in serious trouble and put in juvenile hall. The judge ordered the mother to attend parenting classes and suggested ours. She was very hostile.

"What's your name?" I asked her.

"My name doesn't matter," she snapped. "I live too far to go to your parenting classes. Do you have any classes closer?"

I said, "I'm sorry, I don't. I suggest you look into adult education or some of the clinics."

"No! I'm just not going to go. I'll get a doctor's excuse. My back is bad. I can't sit for more than twenty minutes. How long are your classes?"

"Two hours," I said.

"That's impossible. I can't possibly sit for two hours." I told her that the judge probably wouldn't return her daughter until she'd completed the classes. This was standard procedure.

She responded sarcastically, "His Royal Highness will just have to accept my doctor's excuse. I know I've made mistakes. It started at birth. I bailed her out when she needed discipline. I told her teachers not to discipline her, so now she thinks she can do anything she wants. I didn't make the same mistakes with my younger son. I read the books and went to classes. This is ridiculous. I suppose this class costs money, too. Well, I'm not going to pay. I took her to a judge because she was uncontrollable, and now his Royal Highness thinks that I'm the one who's at fault."

I interrupted the diatribe by saying, "Mother, you need help. You could benefit from going to counseling."

"*Who* needs help?"

"*You* do, Mom," I repeated calmly.

She hung up after having the last word, "I didn't make this call to be insulted. Good-bye."

Here's a rock-solid parenting secret—following the motto "Give children whatever they want" is bound to bring trouble; children need to have reasonable rules and boundaries. When you're responsibly "in control," your children feel safe. This is much more important to them than letting them have their own way.

Permissive parents may not know how to make firm statements of rules and set boundaries. They usually lack assertiveness skills. They ask their child, "Isn't it time for you to go to bed now?" "Are you going to get ready for school?" "Don't you think you should eat some vegetables?" In these instances and others, too, children need to be firmly but respectfully told rather than asked about what's to be done.

When discussing their children, "buddy parents" express helplessness. "No matter what I do, he won't mind me." These parents don't take charge, and they see themselves as victims. And the children of permissive parents have an inflated sense of what is rightfully theirs. They don't learn to treat others with respect.

In childhood we develop habits that last a lifetime. Children often don't understand what's best for them. Growing up is a slow process which takes a minimum of twenty years. Children need guidance to develop their thinking, their ability to love and care for others, and to be confident. They need to be carefully taught right from wrong. By neglecting to provide direction, to set limits and to follow through assertively, the permissive parent prevents children from reaching their potential as responsible, mature adults able to get along with others. Avoid misguided love in the form of permissivism. Instead, substitute discipline with love.

The Perfectionist: Nothing Is Ever Good Enough

The *perfectionist* expects flawless performance. The attitude is "If you're not perfect, you're not good enough." Perfectionists continually aspire to unrealistic goals. They can be so critical that their children despair of ever succeeding. The truth is that perfection exists only in the abstract, not in real life. No parent, child, or family is ever perfect. Because nothing ever meets their high standards, these parents lead miserable lives, and they make their children miserable, too. Perfectionists would do well to replace perfection with quality, excellence, or any personal best which is a reachable goal. They need to realize that mistakes aren't so horrible. In fact, we all learn valuable lessons from our mistakes.

Sometimes a parent is both the boss and a perfectionist, a very difficult combination for a child. I was glad that Jessie and Efrim were in the same Parent Connection class. They needed to learn similar lessons. Efrim's son, Shawn (13), is a straight-A student and a star athlete in junior high school. Efrim is a harsh taskmaster who keeps a tight reign on Shawn and is quick to point out his mistakes. Although everyone admires Shawn for being a "super jock" and he's popular at school, he bites his nails severely and frequently has nightmares of failure.

He's painfully aware every time he doesn't do something right and worries constantly about what his father is going to say if he doesn't measure up. In fact, he's in a perpetual state of anxiety about failure. No matter what he achieves, it isn't enough.

The Chip-Off-the-Old-Block

Another version of the perfectionist is the parents who identify with their children too closely. This is the *chip-off-the-old-block* problem. Their attitude is, "My child is just like me." It's yet another form of misguided love. For example, Jessie isn't satisfied with Willie unless he becomes a super athlete, and Efrim won't settle for anything but perfect performance with Shawn. Both fathers feel that they missed out and are making darn sure that their sons don't miss out, too. They even refuse to tolerate any interests their sons have that differ from their own plans.

Another example of a chip-off-the-old-block is a mother who drives her daughter to become an acclaimed actress. The daughter would rather be an artist than an actress. And there are endless parent-child variations of this same theme. Chip-off-the-old-block parents prevent their children from developing in ways that are natural to them.

Each person is unique. When parents don't allow their children to become independent, free-thinking individuals, the result may be low self-esteem and lack of confidence, or a distorted sense of reality. Children should be allowed to grow and follow whatever reasonable, socially-acceptable interests satisfy them. They have a right to develop their natural potential without being forced to live up to unreasonable parental demands.

The Abusive Parent—Not Me!

Being a parent is an awesome responsibility. Few adults are trained to be parents. We rely mostly on what our parents did. I've found parents that routinely abuse and neglect their children who think that it's "those other awful people" who do that.

People with an active conscience routinely examine their actions for excesses in corporal or psychological punishment. The *abuse* definition used in this book is "to cause another pain or suffering." It's easy to get busy or frustrated with your own life. *Neglect* happens when we let important things slide with our children, when it would be better to take action.

We need to demystify the negatively-charged issue of child abuse and neglect. I see abuse and neglect on a continuum or as a matter of degree. Responsible, well-meaning parents make mistakes and resort to both at times. Feeling guilty doesn't solve the situation, but taking constructive action with your children does.

When I was actively parenting my sons, I was keenly aware of the temptation to get excessive with them. Abuse and neglect was a way of life with Robert and TJ. They expected it. They thought my husband and I were weak because we couldn't measure up. I know in my heart of hearts that I was capable of some degree of abuse and neglect with them. Families can be hotbeds of stress and can easily get out of control. Ours was no different. My husband and I learned to build in checks and balances to keep relationships with our sons in balance. It's easy to sweep abuse and neglect under the rug and think, Not me. It's better to think, Yes, I'm capable of both, so what am I going to do about it?

The very worst way to raise children is with abuse and neglect. Abusive parents harm their children physically and psychologically by doing and saying things that hurt them. They take out their frustrations on their children. They may use excessive corporal punishment or be verbally aggressive. These are parents who rarely understand the developmental stages and phases of childhood. Like others who subscribe to the "miniature adult syndrome," they expect children to think and act like adults. If the children don't, they chastise them.

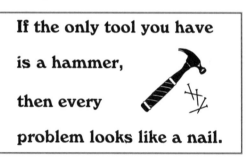

If the only tool you have is a hammer, then every problem looks like a nail.

Abusive, neglectful parents have few skills. They're unfamiliar with the variety of techniques they could use to correct their children's problem behavior. *If the only tool you have is a hammer, then every problem looks like a nail.* Many parents pound their children, sometimes to death.

I'm constantly aware of parents who are on the brink of danger with their children. When the phone rings at The Parent Connection, we never know what to expect. One week, a father called and asked if I thought he should send his son, George, to school on Monday. I said, "I don't understand what the problem is. Why wouldn't you send George to school on Monday?" He said that George had lied about stealing some money, and his father's girlfriend had used an extension cord to correct George's behavior. He said, "It wasn't anything that I did, but she left some marks on him, and there are some cuts in three different places. If the school people see it, they'll report it to the authorities. Do you think I should go to a parenting class?"

I said, "Yes, I absolutely think you should go to a parenting class, and you should send your son to school. You need to learn better ways to handle your problems."

"But I didn't do it."

I said, "That's not how the social worker will look at it. A social worker will think that you put your son in jeopardy by moving in with a woman who would abuse him."

"Oh," he said.

"It would look a lot better for you if you would enroll yourself in a parenting class. Social workers aren't interested in removing your children if they think the parents are learning and that the children will be treated safely." Unfortunately, I never heard from the man again. He was another parent who didn't want to give me his name because he thought I might report him to the authorities. Child abuse and neglect are very serious problems. The fact is that a child could be damaged for life as a result. It's a social issue that every parent has an obligation to understand and prevent.

Neglectful Parents Don't Act When They Should

Joanna hadn't sent her ten-year-old daughter to school for almost a year and a half. The authorities had taken the child out of her home. She said, "I just never realized it was that long that she hadn't gone to school. She's sick with colds a lot. I just wanted her home with me. I missed her so much."

This child had no cuts or marks, but her mother's lack of concern and follow through resulted in serious neglect which could have long-reaching consequences.

Adults aren't routinely taught the interpersonal skills that are essential for successful living. The abuse and neglect of children comes from parents' failure to learn basic skills for being organized, managing stress, and communicating effectively. Many of today's parents were abused and neglected as children. Some never learned how to take care of their own basic needs and are therefore not in a position to take care of the needs of others. The way to stop this cycle of disastrous child rearing practices is with an intervention program, one which teaches parents the skills and knowledge they've missed. *A weak person can't be a strong parent.* The Parent Connection shows parents how to be skillful, strong, and nurturing.

Terri voluntarily enrolled in our classes because she was keenly aware that she had been parented badly. Her father died of alcoholism, and her mother was bitter and critical. She knew there had to be a better way to live, she told us. She wanted her baby, Patrick, to have a decent life. In her third class she asked, "Will you teach me how to ignore a six-month-old child?" She got my full attention. She had swelling under her eyes and looked sad and exhausted as she sank into the sofa.

I responded with, "I need more information, Terri. What's going on?"

She told us that her mother, with whom she lived, had terminal cancer. Her mother expected Terri to wait on her and nothing she did was ever good enough. This interfered with Terri's relationship with her infant son. Terri was burned out. She didn't really want to ignore Patrick, but she felt helpless. The class went to work brainstorming with her how to solve her problem. These were some of the things they said:

- Contact the American Cancer Society to see what services they offer.
- Look for volunteers who will drive her mother back and forth for chemotherapy.
- Find counselors who will talk with Terri and her mother about how to get along better.
- Can Terri afford a private nurse?
- Is Terri's mother eligible for a hospice program?

Terri told us that her mother had $250,000 in the bank, which she refused to spend, plus her house and two cars. I was surprised, because Terri was living on welfare. Then we told her to get legal aid.

She agreed that six-month-old babies should not be ignored. She knew this already. As we gave her ideas, I saw the puffiness around her eyes go away, the redness disappear, and her energy come back as she sat straight up and smiled.

I followed Terri for several months. The counselors at the American Cancer Society demanded that her mother be reasonable. Her mother agreed to pay for her nursing care and not to force Terri into doing it. After her mother died, Terri came back to finish the classes.

Terri realized that she didn't know enough to be a good parent. She said, "A parent's responsibility is awesome. I've got a lot to learn." Parenting expertise involves considerable time and self-realization.

Getting Past Guilt

Even parents who have done harmful things or who have ignored and neglected their children can learn to become better parents. Most parents, regardless of how skillful they are, feel guilty over things they did and didn't do. To make progress, they need to put the past behind them, get rid of the guilt, and face the future with confidence.

Everything about Hannah's appearance indicates she's miserable. As she told us, "My son, Dwight (17), is doing a year in juvenile hall for grand theft auto. He wouldn't go to school. Then he and a bunch of boys stayed out all night, and one had some crack. Dwight ended up going along with these older boys."

"How're you doing?" I asked.

"Not very well."

I said, "It looks like you aren't sleeping much."

She was again surprised that I knew this. "No, I don't sleep."

"You're taking this pretty hard."

"I can't believe he would do that. He was such a good boy. He would go to church and was such a help and comfort to me."

"You're thinking that if you'd really been a good parent then Dwight wouldn't have gotten into trouble?"

"Yes. I keep trying to figure out where I failed him."

"Hannah, did you tell Dwight to stop going to school, stay out all night, smoke crack, and steal cars?"

"No, I didn't. I would never tell him that."

"Then what are you guilty of?"

"I don't know. It must be something because he sure went off the deep end."

"Hannah, did you make some mistakes with Dwight?"

"Yes."

"Do you know of any parent who hasn't made mistakes?"

"No."

"You did the best you could with what you had to work with. Right?"

"Well, I guess I did."

That's true for all of us. All parents make mistakes, and so do all children. It's easy to see what we should have done in any situation. What's important is one of the key secrets of good parenting—learn from your mistakes, forgive yourself and your children, then go on to concentrate on solutions rather than problems.

"Hannah, were you standing with Dwight the night he decided to smoke crack and steal that car, whispering in his ear, 'Do it, do it'?"

"No," she laughed.

"Then, it sounds like he made that choice, not you. You aren't guilty of his crime, he is. Instead of blaming yourself for his bad choices, I suggest that you put that energy into forgiving and accepting. The present is more important than the past. Now, how do you feel?"

"Better."

"I suggest that before you go to bed tonight, you say three times, 'I'm innocent, I'm innocent, I'm innocent.' Will you do that?"

"Yes," she said. When we closed the class, Hannah added, "I'm glad I came tonight because I found out that I'm innocent." Everyone in the class spontaneously clapped for her.

As long as Hannah stays stuck in her "guilt," she doesn't actively solve problems. I recommended that she use Dwight's absence as an opportunity to evaluate how her life was going. I asked her what she needed to do to take care of herself. Is Dwight going to come home to the same old mom or a new, improved mom? She asserted that it would be a new, improved version.

Hannah continued to improve her parenting skills until she met her requirements for class completion. She called me right after Dwight came home a year later. She had changed to a better job with more money, and had joined an exercise class at the YWCA. She became more active in her church and she took over the Sunday School program when the director became ill. The night she gave up guilt was the night that she began to move forward. Relating to your children from a place of guilt is another form of misguided love.

Ready to Forgive?

You've probably seen some of yourself in this chapter. Most readers will think about their parents, grandparents, or others they know that behaved in a misguided way. They showed their love for their children inappropriately. In fact, you might have questioned if there was any love there at all. By understanding what motivates people to treat others in these misguided ways, a lot of healing can take place within families. You can't do what you don't know how to do. If you or your parents weren't wisely guided as parents, serious mistakes were bound happen. With understanding, people in families can come to forgiveness. Then miracles occur and the Good Life happens. *Who can you forgive today for the misguided way love was shown to you?*

When you understand what people think, how they think, and why they think that way, you can better anticipate your own responses. You'll see yourself, your children, and everyone who's important to you in the next chapter. Please keep an open mind.

♥

CHAPTER SIX

HOW CHILDREN THINK

Have you ever wondered why the younger generation leaves a trail of empties, sticky counter tops, and spilt milk? Children walk right by the trash cans, kick over the empty dog dish, and leave the house with the stereo blaring—all without batting an eyelash of concern. "Don't they see it?" parents wail. Actually, they don't, and that's a key parenting insight—children are programmed to see what's *right* before they see what's *wrong;* parents see what's wrong before they see what's right. Why is this?

The phenomenon is easily explained by the "pleasure/pain" principle. As we said earlier, all people want to experience more pleasure than pain. However, children are tuned into what is pleasurable in a way that we're not.

Take ten-year-old Kirk. When he comes home from school, he's hungry. His immediate thought is to make a peanut butter and jelly sandwich. At the critical point when the sandwich is made, what does Kirk think is right to do? Eat the sandwich, of course.

Everybody knows that children can do more than one thing at once. What's right to do next is turn on the TV set. During the commercial break, he realizes that he's thirsty. As he pours a glass of milk, he hears that the commercial is over. He rushes back to the living room so as not to miss the program. His mind is fully absorbed in the show when his parents walk in.

What is the first thing that they see? Kirk is glued to the "boob tube" while the milk is left out, the refrigerator door is open, and the peanut butter and jelly jars are on the counter top along with the remnants of his sandwich on the sticky knife. "What's the matter with that boy?" It never occurred to Kirk to put it all away. He was too busy satisfying his immediate needs. He wouldn't see what's wrong at all if his parents didn't point it out.

Grown-ups have a heavy burden that children, by their nature, don't notice. Call it "responsibility, duty, and obligation." Adults often get more pleasure by maintaining an established order, seeing that everyone is safe, that there's food in the house, and that the bills are paid. They also want to know that everyone is doing his or her share. Children stay children for a long time, because they have adults to worry for them. If they didn't, they might grow up too fast and put us out of a job!

An important breakthrough for parents is when they understand the dramatic differences in how adults and children think. Understanding these differences helps strengthen bonding and understanding between you and your children. This knowledge will help you have a great relationship with your children.

Play is a Child's Work

Pleasure is critically important to children. They develop "thinking skills" when they decide which activity will be more "fun." Jean Piaget, the great Swiss researcher who studied the developmental stages of children, is famous for saying, "Play is a child's work." Children need opportunities for different types of play. They need structured, supervised play, and they also need situations where they can think independently.

Children naturally look for ways to have fun. Pleasure is what motivates them. The way to get them to do what you call "work" is to make it fun, and it will be hard for them to resist.

All People Want More Pleasure than Pain

When you woke up this morning, did you ask yourself, "How much pain can I have today?" No one does! Inviting pain goes against our primary motivation. Yes, pain is part of life, but we're all neurologically programmed to try our best to avoid it. *All people want more pleasure than pain.* Think about how you've organized your life so that your needs are regularly met. You live in a home with comfortable conveniences around you, you have a source of income so that you can buy the basics, and you probably have a car or some means of covering distances where you can't easily walk. In fact, you probably have gone beyond your basic needs to add some extras to enhance your pleasure. It's important to think about how you manage your life in order to have more pleasure than pain. This can help you understand your child's behavior.

Human beings aren't the only creatures with a primary motivation to experience more pleasure than pain. All living things have this agenda. They have adapted to ways that enable them to survive and live optimally. The lofty redwood grows hundreds of feet tall so that its uppermost branches will be able to absorb sunlight. A gazelle has well-developed legs for outrunning predators, a fish will swim toward a food supply, and a cactus will store plenty of water during a wet winter in preparation for a long dry spell. Likewise, children are continuously exploring ways to have fun. They need your guidance to understand what will ultimately enhance their lives, rather than merely satisfy this moment's curiosity.

Why Did You Do It?

Mom and Dad tell Buddy (5) he can play outside while they finish getting ready for church. Buddy is warned, "Don't get wet!" But when his parents are ready to leave twenty minutes later, they're dismayed to see that he's soaked from splashing in puddles. "Why did you do it?" they ask incredulously.

Have you ever asked a child, "Why did you do it?" The answer you probably got was intended to deflect personal blame, something like, "I don't know." Most children have learned not to say, "I did it because it was fun," which is exactly why they do anything. Children are highly tuned into what gives them pleasure.

It had rained for a week, and this was the first time Buddy had been able to play outside. He found all sorts of exciting things to do in the fresh, crisp air. He didn't notice that he was getting wet, because he was having too much fun. He wasn't purposely "disobeying" his parents.

The fact that Buddy is now wet, and it's time for church, doesn't give his parents pleasure. Rather than make this situation worse, they could simply tell him, "Buddy, you were told not to get wet because we wanted you to be ready for church now. You need to change quickly to dry clothes so that we can go." Mom and Dad might handle the situation differently next time by anticipating that the pleasure of playing outside after a rainstorm would far outweigh his ability to stay dry, and keep him inside a few more minutes.

When parents understand that play is a child's work, they don't have to ask, "Why did you do it?" That line of questioning invites power struggles. Many parents would assume that Buddy was purposely bad, just to push his parents' buttons. This example shows that children are far more motivated to have fun than they are to remember a parent's instructions.

Parents are at a breakthrough point when they understand that the pleasure children find in play activities is their primary motivator. Historically, many people thought a child should act like a responsible adult—but they were wrong. The best method for helping children develop appropriately is to "catch them being good" when they behave well, divert them when they're not, and provide them with opportunities to develop their natural abilities. Another valuable method is to pare down distractions to your children which aren't in their best interests (for example, controlling the amount of explicit sex and violence your children see on TV and in movies).

The way that successful parents work with their children's natural motivation to play is to pay attention to those good things that they're naturally attracted to. A lot of power struggles can be avoided by this method. Parents can use this knowledge to build more peace and joy in their families.

One of the joys of having children is the opportunity it gives adults to play like a child again. Take time to play with your children; it's one of the best things you can do for them. They need many multisensory activities and toys to play with. Provide opportunities for your children to learn many different life skills that will enrich their lives: swimming, bicycling, roller skating, horseback riding and sports, to name a few. Learning to play computer games, teaching children to type, solving puzzles and mysteries, and reading on a regular basis will greatly enrich their lives. Travel, sightseeing, movies, and amusement parks add zest to the parent-child relationship. Observe and develop holiday traditions and celebrate special events like birthdays. Think of ways to create happy memories for your children, and they'll forever thank you for it.

Many fathers are finding out how much fun it is to play with their children. When my father was well into his senior years, he told me that his one regret was that he didn't take more time to play with his children when we were growing up. He thought that the most important thing he could do was to work hard to support us financially. He was rarely home, and when he was, he was tired. Today's trend is healthier—fathers are living a more balanced life. Children need their fathers, and fathers need their children.

A Child's Sense of Time

Adults in our culture measure time in very sophisticated ways. We order our lives by the clock. We think about the past, and project what we think the future will be like. Children, however, think about time very differently.

Young children experience time only in the present. They've actually had very little past to use as a reference. They don't understand history or the future. Everything for them is immediate. Young children want what they want right now. They're not able, without training, to delay immediate gratification. They have to be trained to eat dessert after dinner and not before, to stop playing to take a bath, or to watch TV after they've finished their chores. They don't want to save money now for something more expensive later. This is *adult* behavior.

Older children also experience time in the present. How many teenagers do you know that carry an appointment book with them? Teenagers don't plan much. Most of their activities are last minute, which is why proximity to a telephone is critical to them. How else can they keep track of where the action is?

Often a child's orientation toward the present clashes with a parent's orientation toward the future. For example, adults want to keep children in school so that they can be prepared for the future, but it's a future children really don't understand. Most children haven't figured out the connection between doing well in school today and living a more satisfying life later. It takes maturity and experience to look ahead and plan.

Which takes us to another parenting insight—the way to keep children growing up responsibly (and keep them in school, too) is by appealing to their immediate sense of fun and belonging. If you do this with your children, you'll keep their attention long enough to teach them right from wrong and grow up to be "R=TLC."

There is a corollary to this parenting insight—children don't learn well in a hostile environment. Think of a class you took where you intensely disliked the teacher. Is this the class where you learned the most? Was that your favorite subject? Not likely. Children learn best in a positive environment where the teacher or parent is reliable, sensitive, and trusted.

The Six Stages of Loving

The ability to love develops gradually for all people. Children go through six distinct stages as their ability to love and to think morally and ethically develops. A child needs to develop thoroughly in each stage before moving on to the next. Once you understand the stages, you can appreciate what your children are doing or not doing rather than becoming frustrated. You'll make allowances for their immaturity and let them progress at their own pace while you guide them toward R=TLC. You can also pinpoint which stage your children are at and help them build a sturdy foundation so that they'll be prepared to move to the next stage.

I've used the work of Jean Piaget and Lawrence Kolhberg in defining the six distinct stages that children move through in learning how to love or develop moral and ethical thinking. These two great philosophers were the first to identify and promote these important concepts.

First, we'll discuss what to expect when children develop optimally, including the most probable time frames for each stage. Later, I'll explain what happens when development is arrested or stopped at any one of these stages and what happens when these children become adults.

STAGES OF LOVING

6	UNIVERSE	ADULT
5	SOCIETY	15+
4	LAW & ORDER	12–15
3	FAIRNESS	7–11
2	PLEASING OTHERS	4–6
1	SELF	B–4

Concrete Thinking: Steps 1–2   Abstract Thinking: Steps 3–6

STAGE ONE: Loving Oneself—Ego (Birth to Age 4)

"I should get my own way." At this stage, children are developing their ego or sense of self. They learn to love themselves. Children at this age have no sense of pleasing others. Their primary interest is in doing what they want to do when they want to do it. They strongly object to being told "No." They don't want to share because they don't understand giving. It is important to understand a child's need for repetition at this stage. Each time your children hear the same story, watch the same video or engage in the same activity, their learning increases. This is a child's most vulnerable time. They expect to have their needs taken care of automatically. Children at this age lack the ability to think beyond their immediate needs. They don't think about the past and they have no sense of the future.

At this stage, children are developing their survival skills. Children are "good" so that they can get rewards and avoid punishments—more pleasure than pain. They have no inclination to please others; they're too busy learning how to feel good in their environment. Bonding with a consistent, loving caretaker is vitally important for young children. They become attached to those who cuddle and care for them. Sponge-like, they absorb their surroundings in an uncritical way. If they're treated roughly, or if their basic needs aren't provided for in a timely fashion, they quickly absorb the idea that "I'm not good enough or worthy of love." The important concept of "love of self" can be jeopardized or reinforced at this stage.

The foundation for a child's lifetime is set in place in these years, mostly by their parents and other caregivers. Many parents label the self-absorbed characteristics of this stage as being bad, selfish, or spoiled. It's important for parents to understand this stage of human development, for without a healthy, loving sense of self, a child cannot have a successful life.

Most experts in child development agree that a child's fundamental personality is formed well before age five. By this time a child is keenly aware of "Who I am." "Am I smart or am I dumb? Am I friendly or unfriendly? Am I ugly or good-looking? Am I rich or poor?"

By now, children have figured out where they live and what their culture is. Because children think literally, with sharp contrasts, there's no room for a partial interpretation. They see in black and white. They think all or nothing. They hear yes or no. Shades of gray and "maybe" don't fit into their logic. This is why prudent parents will be careful to set a positive feeling tone in the family, catch their children being good, and make child labels positive rather than negative.

Stage Two: Loving to Please (Ages 4 to 6)

At this stage, children recognize that grown-ups are the "authority" and they think, I should do what I'm told. Children begin to realize that by pleasing others, they'll get more of what they want when they want it. Their motivation is still to get what they want now, only they've developed more finesse. They seek out rewards for good behavior. They like to share their successes. We hear, "Mommy, look! Daddy, see what I did." There's no more critical time than this stage for you, as a parent, to show your appreciation of your child's small achievements. Your child probably won't remember if you were present for his or her very first step, but your child is keenly aware if you're paying attention now. There are many important first steps in a child's life. Each one deserves acknowledgment.

Remember this parenting secret—success attracts success, failure attracts failure. Avoid catching your child at failure; that's a bad habit. Treat a mistake as an error in judgment, and show your child a better way. Teach right from wrong, and make the rules clear. This stage is critical for developing thinking skills and learning to love others, and the positive, loving example you set for your children will be the best influence possible for them.

At this stage, children want to feel a part of the family by "helping." Children strongly model their parents or caregivers. "I want to be just like Mommy or just like Daddy." They'll stay out of trouble by doing what they think is expected of them. Parents may wish this stage would last forever, but it's over in the blink of an eye. If you manage the first two stages well (Ego and Loving to Please), your children will bond with you, and you'll continue to have an important influence over their thinking and behavior.

Stage Three: Loving Fairness (Early Elementary School Age)

Children begin to realize that rules can help them get more of what they want. Now they're more likely to think, We have our rights, too; parents shouldn't order us around. They're still highly motivated by "I want what I want when I want it," only now they have a stronger "What's in it for me?" attitude. The favor your children so willingly did at Stage Two now will cost you a quarter. At this stage children love to bargain. They question the rules, test the rules, and ignore the rules. You might feel that you're starting all over with what used to be obvious. "When is bedtime? Why can't I play outside after dark?" This is a valuable stage where children are more interested in seeing what they can do with negotiation than they are in having absolute control. Smart parents need to be firm about important rules and look for opportunities to negotiate a deal that's fair for everybody concerned.

At this stage children think, I should look out for myself, but I'll be fair to those who are fair to me. Fairness is interpreted as "I'll scratch your back if you scratch mine." It's the morality of the marketplace. They have little regard for individuals who play by different rules.

At the beginning of this stage, children make up rules for games. In creative play activities, such as playing house or school, rules are made up on the spot. There's considerable testing to see what people will go for. As they begin playing more formal board games, cards or athletics, they continue to experiment. You'll hear "Mommy, he cheated," or, "I'm going to tell my Dad." Eventually, children come to realize that it's better to play by the rules because it's fair. They also learn important lessons in competitive sports from a teacher or coach or referee. Learning to play by the rules is crucial. You don't want your children going through life thinking it's okay to make up the rules as they go along.

STAGE FOUR: Loving Law and Order (Early to Middle Teens)

At Stage Four, children want to be well thought of. They need to belong. Their attention is drawn away from the family to social groups they find at school or in the neighborhood. They conform to the group that they identify with to get social approval. They absorb the expectations of individuals they like and model them.

This stage can be maddening for parents, as they see their own influence over their children eroded by the all-important peer group. The parent thinks the child belongs at home, but the child finds "home" a place to make a pit stop until something better comes along. This is a natural phase that all generations experience in becoming independent. Each new generation follows its own fads in dress, slang and music, finding its own ways to create an identity. One of the biggest issues of the mid-teens is the intense desire to go through the rite of passage of getting a driver's license. Teenagers rightly see this as an important step to their independence.

Another characteristic of this stage is that for the first time children can do *abstract* thinking, instead of being locked in to literal true and false, right and wrong, yes and no polarized thinking. They can think with ideas and can see between the extremes. What used to be a simple negotiation for parents can now be a drawn-out debate about principles. Instead of discussing what's fair, they now argue about rights and justice. "Who are you to tell me what to do? You're being old-fashioned!" Children at this stage are quick to assert their perceived "rights," and tell *you* what the laws are.

In earlier stages, children have been learning about the difference between rules and laws. Rules are more flexible, but some rules are so important that they're laws. We all have to obey them. Most teenagers understand that laws are necessary because without them there would be no order and no safety. They know that we couldn't survive if everyone lied, cheated, and stole. They've seen instances of people being treated unfairly, too, and most understand the value of getting along harmoniously with others.

Many teens have developed a political identity, at least on some issues. They know something about racism, sexism, the abuse and neglect of children, and choice and abortion. In order to make sense of these and other controversies, they join groups which give them definition and help them center their beliefs. At this stage teenagers may become fanatically religious or just as fanatically against religion. They're more sure of themselves as they try on grown-up ideas (which they may rapidly discard once they find another way of believing or acting which seems better). It's at this stage, too, that they develop a more idealistic way of looking at their world, preparing them for Stage Five.

Stage Four people are the backbone of society, because they believe in obeying the laws, paying taxes, and maintaining the social order. They hold strong family values and believe in being of service to the community as well as to their country in time of danger. Every parent wants their children to learn to live in socially-acceptable ways.

STAGE FIVE: Loving One's Society (Late Teens)

In optimal child development, older teenagers accept that there are principles of justice, fairness, and cooperation that build harmony among people. They realize that "I should be responsible to my society and country." Most have had civics classes where they studied the U. S. Constitution and the Bill of Rights. They realize that obeying the law and keeping order is necessary. They are concerned that justice is served and that human rights are fully protected. They're interested in seeing that the greatest good exists for the greatest number. They've come a long way from "What's fair is what I want!"

At this stage, meeting obligations helps children develop self-respect. In the different cultures and economic levels in our society, they see that all people are bound by a unifying order. We can be different, yet are united in loving our country.

Often, there's the chauvinistic belief that "my country is best." Patriotism can make them vulnerable to the political climate of the time. Historically the military drafts young men around age 18 when they're the most idealistic and willing to follow direction. The military satisfies their need to belong to someone or something larger than themselves. In child development, it takes twenty years to reach this degree of thinking, but it won't happen without cultivating the idea of loving something larger than oneself.

STAGE SIX: Loving Universality (Young Adult)

When Edward H. White stepped outside the space capsule in outer space, linked to civilization by only a lifeline, he was unaware that the whole world was collectively holding its breath for fear that he'd be lost forever. His attention was elsewhere. He described the experience of peacefully floating in a dark, noiseless void. In front of him was this jewel called Earth. The gleaming blue water, large land masses, and swirling white clouds were stunning in their beauty. He realized that everything dear to him was located on that magnificent gleaming jewel. He also became aware that there are no boundaries, no imaginary lines that separate one country from another. He saw the interconnectedness of all life, all people, everywhere. He described it as the most mystical experience he ever had.

When pictures of our earth reached home, many of us realized for the first time that we're one. One planet, one people, one biosphere, one universe. This is home.

Stage Six doesn't usually arrive until a person is an adult. Having a universal consciousness, believing that we're one world and one people, requires maturity. Along with this realization comes the belief that all human beings are important and deserve to be treated fairly. "No matter how different people are from me, I respect them and honor their dignity." People at this stage also strive to wipe out injustices in the world and make living conditions better for people far different from themselves.

This consciousness extends beyond human beings. Stage Six thinkers see the interconnectedness of all living beings. Belonging to the complex web of life prohibits cruelty to animals and calls for us to act with care toward the fragile ecosystem we live in. Our role, according to Stage Six individuals, is to protect and not exploit the resources of the earth, including its animals. Their personal job is to protect the environment and the ozone layer, prevent the greenhouse effect, and keep the world's waterways clean and habitable. They see saving the Amazon Rain Forest as an important issue.

Though they may be patriotic, people in Stage Six aren't chauvinistic. They see themselves as citizens of the world. They're good thinkers who are also loving and have the confidence to take the action necessary to make the world better for us all. The Golden Rule of "Do unto others as you would have them do unto you," a rule found in religions and cultures around the world, becomes a moral principle which guides their personal action.

What Can Go Wrong?

Most people have not made it to Stage Six. In fact, very few think on a universal scale. A universal consciousness has to be carefully cultivated. Individuals must actively strive to acquire it. Parents and teachers can only lay the seeds of understanding for it in youth. It entails a level of responsibility that few people can accept, which is one reason the world today is environmentally endangered.

The "average" individual stops growing at Stage Four, the Loving Law and Order stage. Even the most stubborn rebel usually comes to realize that breaking the law isn't worth paying heavy fines or doing jail time. Most people expect to live within the law, and when they don't, they know that there are penalties. Driving drunk means having a license pulled, not paying tickets means having them go to warrant, and stealing means getting arrested and paying restitution. We have laws to protect us from the lawless, otherwise there would be no order. Life wouldn't be worth living if people stayed in the early stages of childhood, if everyone tried to have whatever they wanted whenever they wanted it, regardless of who got hurt. The meanest and toughest criminal element would take over, leaving the rest of us with little say over our lives.

Most people understand the need for an orderly society. Yet countless others don't care about people outside of themselves. They're adults who think like children because they're stuck in one of these earlier stages. The Six Stages can help us understand these problems.

The Sociopath

Some people never leave Stage One, the stage where we learn self-love. We learn to survive here. We learn to attract rewards and avoid pain. Countless people are stalled at this stage. They grow up still thinking like little babies. "Me, me, me." They haven't even progressed to Stage Two people pleasing.

It's easy to be fooled by their intentions. When they're still young and cute, people affectionately call them "con-artists." As they get older, they can be charming. They know just what to say so you'll open your wallet, give them a meal, provide a place to stay, lend your car, and whatever else they need.

Sociopaths have learned the lingo of "borrow, pay you back right away, I'll help, you're so kind, I'll appreciate you forever," and so on. They have an endless array of ways to convince you to give them something. However, all the giving is one way—the sociopath only takes and takes and takes. Their goal is to make you feel good about giving so that they can keep you on tap. Eventually, the tap runs dry. Promises are broken. The borrowed money isn't paid back, the work is left undone, and your "friend" has gone off to easier pickings.

Do you know anyone like that? We all do. Sociopaths don't have "enlightened self-interest." They're only "self-interested." Their concern is all for their own welfare, not for yours. This is how a young child behaves, and this is normal behavior for them. We gladly give to a baby, but we expect the baby will grow up to want to please others, consider what's fair, and respect the law. A sociopath is unable to experience empathy and sympathy. Sociopaths don't have a moral conscience, which means they don't understand how what they do or say affects other people.

Sociopaths rarely change. Their scams work for them, so they don't see any reason to change. The truth is they don't *really* know how to please people. They don't know what's fair beyond "I should get what I want when I want it." They don't understand that the law and their own sense of order lies in self-gratification. They're not holding anything out on you; they don't have anything to give you. This is the important realization—you must understand that they don't know a better way. Saying that they should "do better" is useless. If you must deal with a sociopath, it's better to accept what *is* than to try to wish it away. If you understand the problem, you can protect yourself.

Sociopaths are not usually violent people. They tend to use the "soft touch" to get what they want. If you say "No," they move on to the next likely prospect, and there are plenty of them. They don't do without much, because so many people are gullible and eager to "help." The appropriate response to a sociopath is "No." If you feed their dysfunction, it continues.

When babies don't bond with an adult in their earliest impressionable years, they don't develop the ability to understand how to lovingly give and take. Young children need a stable place to live and constant 24-hour care by consistently loving caretakers. This will optimize the bonding process and allow children to leave Stage One. Children can't learn to feel for others unless they've had someone who has felt for them in their earliest years.

People Pleasers that Are Not Okay

Unfortunately, large numbers of people never get beyond Stage Two people pleasing. They've learned that it feels good to be helpful and make people happy. Now, you may be asking, "What's wrong with that?" Plenty! If a person is stuck in Stage Two, they'll never mature to Stage Three and be concerned about what's fair and what the rules are. People pleasers are only programmed to serve.

As parents, their serving may mean preventing their youngsters from growing up to be independent, responsible adults. Several groups exist to help individuals with this problem. Some are Co-dependency or "Coda" Groups, and the Anonymous programs offer Alanon or Alateen. If Stage Two describes you as an adult, you'll never regret getting help to progress to the other stages.

Guess who's looking for the people pleasers? The sociopaths, of course. The people pleasers are "easy pickings." They give and give, and when the sociopath is displeased, they blame themselves for not doing more and they give some more. I've seen some bizarre marriages between sociopaths and people pleasers. There are also some inappropriate relationships between parent and child in families where no one ever grew up. Such families are never really happy, yet no one has a clue about what's wrong. What's wrong is that no one understands how to be fair.

People pleasers are often women. Female children have traditionally been heavily indoctrinated to please others. Being female once meant having to suffer and be deprived. Fortunately, the social expectations of women and girls are changing to help them understand what's fair and then act accordingly.

Plenty of men are stuck in the people pleaser stage, too. They please the boss, their peers and colleagues, as well as family members. They're the "soft touch" dads. People pleasing is charming in young children, but adults who want to live a full and responsible life need more sophisticated thinking skills.

Fairness Gone Wrong

Gangs and gangsters function at Stage Two and Stage Three. At Stage Two are the "Wannabes" or young people who want to please and to belong, especially when their needs are not adequately met at home. The "Old Gangsters" are at Stage Three. Remember that at this stage, "What's fair is what I say is fair. If you don't like the way the game is played, then you can take your marbles and go home." The Old Gangsters make up the rules, and the Wannabes are eager to learn them. Theirs is a culture of lawlessness. People who are developmentally at the Loving Fairness stage don't understand the law. The only order they accept is what they make up or accept as right. This way neighborhoods are divided into arbitrary "turfs." Specific colors, like red and blue, are associated with particular neighborhoods, schools, churches, and other institutions in the "hood." The people making up the "rules" can now designate that no one from another color or hood may step into their territory without fearing for their lives. This kind of thinking escalates drug trafficking, prostitution, delinquency, other crimes, and social problems. Not *every* Old Gangster is at Stage Three; plenty of them are sociopaths.

An example of fairness gone wrong, taken to extremes, is found in any cluster of people who abide by rules made up by a leader and imposed upon others who don't know how to question whether the rules are fair or not. Street gangs, cults, and organized hate groups are examples of this problem.

People who are stuck at the Loving Fairness stage still think that "I should have what I want when I want it." The made-up rules they play by are intended to give personal advantage. It's a way of manipulating others so they always win. One of the purposes for teaching children games, sports, and other forms of competition is to expose children to predetermined rules. Their attention gradually shifts from "What I say goes" to the rule book, the coach, or the parent who is the higher authority on how to play the game fairly. (This, of course, also has its limitations in cases where rules may be applied cruelly just because they're the rules.)

Taking time to help children expand their thinking about what's fair as something more than "What I want" is going to be a help, not only to the children, but to all the rest of us. Carefully nurturing children through the Six Stages of Loving isn't difficult when you consider the payoff and the penalties. The penalties are all the things that can go wrong when people are arrested at the early stages, especially before they at least learn to respect and obey the law.

Law and Order Used Against People

When people are stuck at Stage Four, however, other problems occur. One is rigidity about the law. The law becomes the highest good, as opposed to principled thinking. "If it's the law, you have to obey it—no exceptions." Certain people fail to see that laws are subject to interpretation. This is why we have judges, people who interpret the law. Some individuals are too ready to condemn, also unwilling to forgive. Some political and religious groups encourage rigid, black and white thinking, never tolerating shades of gray, never leaving room for interpretation or individual circumstances.

My Country Over All

People at Stage Five can be rigid on a more expansive level. They believe "My country is the best country on earth. Others aren't good enough." This flag-waving chauvinism is exclusionary and condones the idea that people who are different aren't okay, are inferior, or aren't worthy of fairness and respect.

There's an inclination toward being single-minded and not realizing that those who live in another part of the world have much in common with ourselves. It's this kind of thinking that has led to perpetual conflict between countries. There are political theorists who believe that this nationalistic thinking contributed to the Cold War for many decades.

Good Luck in Settling Here with Universal Love

It's only at Stage Six that people reach the expansive thinking that's not exclusionary. People at this stage think in technicolor, not in black and white. Differentiations between "me and you" and "right and wrong" are more subtle. Life is rich and full of meaning. Life offers plenty to do. There's no time to be bored.

I've found that when parents in The Parent Connection classes understand how children think, they become more tolerant of their children's behavior. They have a better grasp of how to encourage their children's growth to the next stage. Many parents recognize what stage they're functioning at and realize that there's much more for them to do. People who have made it to Stage Six are more satisfied with their lives and with their children. These are the people who know how to live the Good Life.

❤

CHAPTER SEVEN

SELF-ESTEEM AND CONFIDENCE BUILDING

The importance of protecting your child's self-esteem is one of the greatest parenting breakthroughs in the twentieth century. The most critical time to build self-esteem is before age five, in your child's earliest formative years. Self-esteem was overlooked for centuries because it's a mental state and not something that an untrained eye can easily observe. Successful parents attend to building their children's self-esteem every day.

You Keep the F; I'll Keep My Dream

Monte Roberts is the son of an itinerant horse trainer. Although Monte was rarely in the same school for more than a few months at a time, he caught on quickly when he was there and got good grades.

When he was in high school, his teacher, Mr. Russo, assigned students to draw a plan and write a story of their life dream. Monte submitted an illustration of a 4,000 square foot ranch house on 200 acres and a story describing the race horses he wanted to breed, train, and show. He was astonished to see an "F" and a "See me" when he got his paper back.

Mr. Russo told him that the F was to get his attention. He wanted to spare Monte great disappointments in life. Given his history of moving so often and his parents being poor, the chances that Monte would realize such a grand dream were remote. He asked him to redo the assignment and be more realistic. He sent him away with "Talk it over with your parents."

Though confused, Monte did as he was told. His father listened and thought it over. He said, "Monte, this is one thing I can't advise you on. It's up to you." His mother said, "I believe there are no limits to what you can do if you really make up your mind to doing it."

He thought hard about redoing his paper, but couldn't come up with anything to replace his dream. On Monday morning he took the same assignment back to his teacher, saying, "Mr. Russo, you keep the F; I'll keep my dream."

Today Monte lives his dream in the Santa Ynez Valley of California at "Flag Is Up Farms." He told me that twenty years later after he had graduated from high school, Mr. Russo paid a visit with a tour busload of his friends. He told them all, "Here's a man I told not to go for his dreams when he was a boy. I'm glad that he didn't listen to me."

Through their own shortsightedness, many parents and teachers discourage children from their dreams. Countless children do as they're told and give up on their dreams. Monte is an exception. Although his parents couldn't give him a lot materially, they made up for it by teaching him values and providing encouragement so his self-esteem could grow.

What is Self-Esteem?

People with high self-esteem have an abundance of confidence. Failure doesn't slow them down. When one door closes, they expect another to open. Also, they're tenacious, and their stick-to-it thinking keeps them motivated and progressing. They feel exuberance over a raise or a promotion. They view the day-to-day rewards of life as something they deserve. They are their own cheering squad. Instead of thinking, This is all I deserve, they say, "Hooray for me!" and look forward to the next reward. They see life as alive and exciting. People with good self-esteem have an abundance of confidence. They love themselves. There's a deep knowingness that they're worthy and desirable.

People with high self-esteem see themselves as worthy regardless of what other people think. Self-esteem enables them to keep going under the worst of circumstances. If you see setbacks as temporary and if you practice good coping skills such as managing stress and avoiding self-destructive behavior, you'll weather the storm. The sun always comes out again and fair weather returns. There's an even greater benefit. These "storms" can build character and strength in those people committed to personal growth.

Who Do You See When You Look in the Mirror?

People with self-esteem see beauty and experience goodness all around them. Self-esteem reflects back and radiates out to others. If you see a worthy individual in your mirror, you're more likely to see others as having worth, too. If you lack self-esteem, you're more likely to miss the good in others. You'll see misery whether it exists or not. For you, the cup will be half empty, not half full. The danger is that parents without self-esteem or a positive outlook run the risk of discouraging children, who are particularly vulnerable.

Monte's teacher may have had dreams he had abandoned. Surely it was from love that he advised Monte to be more realistic. Later, Mr. Russo had the courage to face Monte in front of his friends and say, "I made a mistake."

Monte's parents couldn't tell him how to realize his dream but they kept the door open for him to pursue it! He was a good thinker and had confidence in his convictions. In spite of adversity, he tenaciously stuck to what would be a Good Life for him.

Parents who follow the simple formula R=TLC empower their children to rely on the original thinking they'll need when faced with opportunities and difficulties parents cannot possibly anticipate. The way to prepare your children for a future that you don't understand is to build positive character traits while they're still young.

Take Aim and Shoot Yourself in the Foot

People with low self-esteem don't see themselves as having value or as being good enough just the way they are. When opportunities present themselves, they think, I don't deserve it, and then they find ways to sabotage their chances. The result can be a life of missed opportunities and continual disappointment. When other people find them worthy, they think, If you really knew me, you wouldn't like me. They "shoot themselves in the foot" precisely when they need to take a big step forward.

After hearing he had a promotion, Harry became ill with colitis. When Jason started to feel good, he became naughty and tested his parents' limits. Sam had a good marriage but wrecked it with an extramarital fling. Jessica has four As and one C but all she could think about was the C.

Many people live out their lives almost dead, having long ago lost the juices needed to fuel their self-esteem and confidence. The tragedy is that they may have been victimized as children by well-meaning adults, like Monte's teacher, who wanted to "save" them from disappointment.

Most Children Enter Adulthood with Insufficient Self-Esteem

According to self-esteem expert, Jack Canfield, studies show that children entering school in kindergarten have self-esteem measuring 80% and above. As time goes by, they measure less and less. High school seniors measure under 20%, and girls average less than boys! People with low self-esteem lack the confidence to pursue their dreams. They may not even dare to have dreams. People with low self-esteem fail to see that they can make choices which will effect their lives. They don't see themselves as being in charge. Instead, life is something that happens to them.

Taking Action Means Having Confidence

Self-esteem gives us the power to *act* on what we believe. No dream was ever realized without taking action. The decision to act requires confidence. People solve their problems by getting facts, talking to experts, examining their options, and finding strategies to make their dreams real. When confidence is combined with good thinking, answers to problems appear.

When you shoot a roll of film in your camera, do you expect every "take" to be perfect, or do you expect that there will be a "miss" on some of the pictures? A "mis-take" (mistake) is what happens when you *miss* in something you *take* to be a good idea. Mistakes happen when people don't have enough information. They guess or try out an idea. Afterward, when they see the result, they have more information, and they can design a better plan. Too many people don't understand mistakes; they see them as failure. Meanwhile, others view them as an opportunity to learn and grow. Good photographers will examine the mistakes to figure out what went wrong. This is the way that exceptional photographs come into existence. Mistakes make some people even more determined and confident, but this isn't possible without positive self-esteem.

Self-Esteem Builds Confidence

Historically, few parents understood the relationship between self-esteem and confidence building. Today more is known about the importance of self-love or valuing oneself. Which leads us to a parenting secret— knowledgeable parents today want to enhance their children's self-confidence by raising their self-esteem.

Because parents are such powerful role models, what parents say and do has a lasting effect on the child's young psyche. Parents who see themselves as failures will project failure on their children. Those who view themselves as successes are quick to praise their children and to "catch them being good."

Child development specialists believe that the first five years of a child's life are critical, because so much of a child's personality and character is established during this time. The process begins at birth. Personality formation has a lot to do with what you believe about the kind of person you are. If a parent leans toward a negative rather than a positive evaluation, a child is likely to develop a negative rather than a positive interpretation of "Who am I?" Of course, the opposite is also true. A positive self-image comes from a person's learning that he or she is worthy, important, and competent. A lifetime commitment to a particular lifestyle is probable by the time most children walk into their first classroom. Attitudes toward school, learning in general, and caring for others are all established very early in a child's life.

Parents are the First and Foremost Teachers of Children

As we've said earlier, no other person has the influence over a child's future than we do. The skills of parents are critical because they influence long-term outcome. This makes our role as parents a very responsible one indeed. A child's self-esteem is built largely on the "labels" of character that you and other caregivers use to describe that child.

One of the great-grandfathers of parent education, Hiam Ginot, was fond of saying, "Beware that the diagnosis doesn't become the disease." He meant that if you diagnose your aches and pains yourself, you may be wrong—but ultimately your diagnosis may invite the disease. Children absorb descriptions of personality in many subtle ways. Ginot wisely advised parents not to invite the disease of laziness, cheating, stealing, or slovenly behavior by diagnosing a child as having those diseases.

If a parent sees a child as ugly, clumsy or not very smart, that parent is encouraging homeliness, awkwardness, or dullness. What labels did your parents use to describe you? Did the diagnosis become the disease?

Some parents say that they're careful to tell the "truth" since being too positive is unrealistic. This can be a serious mistake, since the "truth" is often subjective and relates to how we feel at the moment. It's better to diagnose on the positive side and watch as the child lives up to what you say by becoming a confident person with high self-esteem.

There are many all-too-common labels that parents use to describe their children. Here are a few of them:

NEGATIVE	**vs.**	**POSITIVE**
ugly	vs.	beautiful
dumb, stupid, slow	vs.	bright, intelligent, smart
foolish, silly	vs.	fun-loving, good-humored
lazy, slow, dull	vs.	busy, hard working, quick
sloppy, dirty, careless	vs.	neat, clean, organized
shy, withdrawn	vs.	friendly, outgoing, likable
naughty, bad, spoiled	vs.	well-behaved, good, well-mannered
an animal, donkey, pig	vs.	a human being, a person
pest, nuisance, monster	vs.	lovable, a joy

How parents, the most powerful people in a child's life, use these words to describe a child's character in the early years has much to do with what kind of people they'll grow up to be.

Children Are Like Sponges

If you put a dry sponge in old mop water, would the sponge have any choice but to soak up the dirty water? If you put a sponge into clear mountain spring water, would the sponge have any choice but to soak up this water? In many ways, young children are like dry sponges. They soak up what's said and done to them in an uncritical way.

Sue has three painfully shy daughters. When Sue introduced Mandy (7) to Louise at a grocery store, Mandy ducked behind her skirt and hid her head. Sue flushed with embarrassment and said, "She's very shy." Mandy has heard this countless times and is living up to it. There's no reason for her to be different. Shyness has been absorbed as "Who I am."

One reason Sue's children are shy is that she was a shy child, and shyness remains a problem for her. She's unintentionally transferred the diagnosis of her own personality to her daughters, and they've absorbed it without question. They think all right-minded people are...shy!

A plan was formed that Sue would bite her tongue rather than ever describe her children as shy in front of them. Instead, she would substitute an opposite label. When Mandy showed the least overture toward friendliness to others, Sue commented on what a "friendly" person she is. Many times she told Mandy that people "like" her; she's an outgoing person. Gradually, the old designation of "I'm shy" disappeared, and Mandy assumed a new image of herself—"I'm a friendly person. People like me." Sue set a goal that Mandy would be able to say "hello" to Pastor Bob without ducking behind her whenever he greeted them after Sunday service. Soon she did this, and achieving this small goal paved the way for Mandy, and her sisters as well, to be friendly to others. Sue learned how labels can work for us, instead of against us.

It's inevitable that young children come to believe what others say about them. If we avoid negative labels and if we acknowledge those times a child shows positive personality characteristics, our children are more likely to turn out with the character traits that we think are desirable.

Describe the Behavior, Not the Child

Sometimes a parent must also acknowledge bad or undesirable behavior. When a child misbehaves, follow this sure-fire parenting secret—we can avoid doing permanent damage if we remember to describe the behavior and not the child; the *child* isn't bad, only the *behavior* is. Let's consider the behavior of Danny.

Situation I

Danny (4) is bouncing his beach ball in the living room, and his mother, Patti, yells from the next room, "Put the ball away, Danny. You're going to break something." Patti continues her work, and Danny, used to ignoring these orders, continues to bounce his ball. He bounces it very high, and it smashes into Mom's expensive lamp, crashing it to the floor.

Patti rushes into the room and screams, "You stupid idiot. I told you not to play with the ball in the house. Now get out of here. You've done enough damage for one day." Danny's eyes are wide and confused as he leaves the house to escape his mother's wrath.

Was the lamp more valuable than Danny's ego? Did Patti tell him appropriately what the rule was for bouncing the ball? Suppose that she had handled the situation differently...

Situation II

When Danny begins to bounce the ball in the living room, Patti thinks if he knew better he would do better. This mother understands that even though she has explained the rule before, children need repetition. So she stops what she's doing and sits down next to him. She explains, "Danny, there are things in the living room that will break easily. There's a chance that the ball could break something. Balls are for playing with outside. You may either put your ball away or go outside and play with it. Which would you like to do?" Danny chooses to bounce the ball outside and the living room lamp is spared.

Many parents might wonder what to do if Danny disobeys and does break the lamp...

Situation III

On another day, Danny picks up his ball and can't resist the temptation to toss it around the living room. He knows that his mother is outside gardening and is unlikely to hear him. He gives the ball a big bounce and it knocks the lamp over. Hearing the crash, Patti rushes into the house. "Oh no, my favorite lamp is broken. Danny, I told you that the house is not the place to bounce your ball. I'm so upset to see this lamp broken. I want you to go to your room while I clean this up. We'll talk about this later."

An hour later, when Patti felt a little calmer, she went to Danny's room. "Danny, I'd like you to tell me what the problem is."

Danny solemnly said, "I shouldn't have bounced the ball in the living room. I broke the lamp."

Patti said, "We have the rule of bouncing the ball outside so that things in the house won't get broken. I'm still upset about that lamp. I'm going to keep your ball for this week. You can find other toys to play with."

A week later she asked Danny if he wanted his ball back. When he said, "Yes," she asked him to repeat the rule about where the ball is to be used. He was able to say that the ball should be played with outside and not in the house.

Patti asked, "Why do we have that rule?"

"So things won't get broken."

"Good, now you understand. You may take the ball outside."

When Danny came into the house later after playing with the ball outside, Patti followed through by saying, "It looks as if you've learned where to play with your ball now, Danny. I'm glad."

In Situation I, Patti didn't take the time to teach Danny the rule of bouncing the ball outside, not in the house. Yelling at a child (or anyone else, for that matter) is an ineffective way of communicating. It contributes to "mother deafness." Because the important first step of teaching the rule has been neglected, Patti shares in the responsibility for the broken lamp. Furthermore, labeling Danny as a "stupid idiot" is an aggressive attack. Such words at a time like this can cause him to internalize that "I'm not a good person. I'm very dumb." He's being rejected by his mother and is escaping the unpleasantness by going outside until she cools off. Repeated incidents like this are guaranteed to destroy self-esteem.

In Situation II, Danny has been taught the rule. Mother takes charge and sees that he plays with the ball in an appropriate place. In Situation III, Danny chooses to break the rule. Patti rightfully is upset that the lamp she loves is broken and that Danny's behavior was at fault. She handles her anger appropriately by describing how she feels about what's happened and avoids a personal attack. She expresses her dislike for his behavior and removes him from the situation until her anger has subsided. It takes about an hour before she feels she can talk to him about what happened. At this point she asks Danny to explain what's gone wrong to check on his comprehension of the rule. She takes the offending ball away as a consequence.

A week later, Patti follows through by checking to see if he's learned this lesson. He assures her that he has and shows her by using the ball outside. She comments on this right away, reinforcing his understanding of the rule and praising him for obeying it.

Let's summarize this process in a parenting secret—children will develop good self-esteem and the confidence to take positive action when you help them develop a firm sense of right and wrong; children need to know not only what to do but also the reasons why.

Buster's Garden

Murray was attending our classes when he described an incident that had happened over the weekend. Murray has a magnificent succulent garden of over 300 specimen plants which he regularly tends. Buster (3) decided to help his dad trim his plants. When Murray walked out onto the patio he was stunned to see huge pieces of his beautiful plants lying all over the patio and the garden clippers on the ground. He was furious to see the damage that Buster had done.

Murray described the scene to us like this: "I couldn't believe that Buster would purposely destroy my plants. I was furious. I stormed into the house and yelled, 'Buster!' He looked up at me with those wide eyes that said it all. He was ready to run. I stopped cold in my tracks. I don't want my son to be afraid of me.

"I shifted from what I was going to do and said, 'You're not finished out here.' I got a large box from the garage and he helped me gather up the pieces. We got into the car and went to the nursery where we bought root tone, several flats, and potting soil. When we got home, he helped me dip each plant into the root tone and plant them into the prepared flats. We call it Buster's Garden."

When Murray was in a rage, he thought that Buster was purposely being "bad." He saw his plants as being destroyed. He saw a disaster. It's an example of crucializing, making an incident into a crisis. He decided to take a "Wedge of Time" (some "time out" to cool down) and moved into action rather than reaction. When he and his son were driving in the car, he had time to think the situation over. In talking with Buster, he realized that Buster thought that he was helping. He'd seen his father use the garden clippers many times. Murray decided that maybe he had a budding gardener on his hands. As they prepared the flats, he talked to Buster about asking before "helping" like that in the future. Murray decided to teach Buster how to trim the plants so that he could develop a better eye for the task.

I asked Murray if perhaps the garden clippers and other toxic materials used in gardening should be kept out of range of a three-year-old, which he agreed was wise to do. Often, when we react, we don't accept any responsibility for our own contributions to the problem.

One evening Murray proudly walked into class to give me a gift. It was a large planter of succulents. He said, "You can't kill succulents; they just grow and grow." Now I have a living and growing testimony that parent education makes a difference. Fortunately, this dad was able to stop and see how he could make an unhappy experience into something that taught a valuable lesson in a positive way.

Joy's Spelling Words

Joy (8) has had a hard life. Her mother frequently wouldn't send her to school, claiming that she was sick. Joy had come to hate school and never did homework. Her father didn't know she existed until a year ago, when a social worker was able to find him and tell him that he had a daughter. He became very interested in her, and was taking parenting classes to help him get full legal and physical custody of her. In his visits, he learned how to have a special time with Joy doing what she hated most—her homework. She needed a lot of encouragement. One day he told me how he had been applying "catch them being good" to this situation.

He'd learned in class that he would not be doing her a favor by calling attention to her mistakes. He told me that the technique he was using was, "Look Joy, you have six of the letters of this word right. As soon as you move this letter where it needs to go, the whole word will be spelled right." Needless to say, Joy is learning to like doing her homework, and showing to her receptive father all of her "little" successes in school. It's these little successes that will change her negative view into a positive experience of school as her self-esteem rises.

Emphasizing and rewarding the positive can go a long way in building a child's self-esteem, but the very best way I know of is for parents to work on their *own* self-esteem. Too many parents take too dim a view of their successes. "Catch them being good" applies as much to *you* as it does to your child. When was the last time you gave yourself a pat on the back for a job well done? Maybe you need to spend more time appreciating and taking care of your own self-esteem. If you can't take care of your own self-esteem, it's unlikely you'll do a very good job of building up self-esteem in your children. You could be inviting a great breakthrough in your whole family by cultivating a more positive self-image.

Self-esteem is fragile. Even a person with good self-esteem isn't set for life. Everyone has setbacks along the way that threaten self-image. Some of the more serious setbacks are illness, financial reversals, breakup of relationships, and the rebellion of teenage children. Once I heard Zig Ziglar say, "Just because you took a bath once, doesn't mean that you won't ever get dirty again. Self-esteem is like that. It needs regular work to keep it clean and positive. There are a lot of different kinds of 'dirt' out there!"

Self-esteem comes from knowing that you've coped in the past, and that you'll be able to weather the storms and setbacks that come along in the future. The more storms you undergo, the better equipped you'll be. Building self-esteem is a lifelong project for every member of your family.

❤

CHAPTER EIGHT

STRESS MANAGEMENT

What is Stress?

Stress is physical and mental tension resulting from circumstances that put you off balance. The primary cause of stress is not getting your needs met. Whenever you're in stress, you're missing something at the needs level. The normal response that we inherited from our ancestors is the "fight or flight" response—either we'll back off or run away from a perceived danger or rush head long into what we think will solve our problems. This phenomenon I call the Dance of Life, reflecting the many decisions we make daily to keep ourselves balanced and to offset stress.

Needs

A *need* refers to something that you must have. To some degree, your survival is at stake. Needs include food, water, air, shelter, clothes, medical care, sleep and safety; but they also include money, love, affectionate touching, appreciation of others, and time for yourself. When we're very young, we have no choice but to rely on our family for meeting our needs. Growing up, we learn to take care of more needs outside of the family.

A family can be a hotbed of stress, because everyone has needs which must be met at the same time. It isn't easy to take care of your own needs while also juggling the needs of others in the family. In stressful times, parents can easily become self-sacrificial. We'd all like our home to be a place where we are refueled, rested, and rejuvenated so we can go out into the world and succeed in school, in work, and in the community. Terrible problems develop in families when members aren't getting their needs met, however. People start competing with each other. Power struggles escalate. When these things happen, home is no longer a safe harbor. It becomes the opposite.

> **A NEED is something you have to have.**
>
> **A FAMILY is where every person's needs are met.**

Anger is a Secondary Emotion

When we're deprived of our needs, we become angry. Anger, however, is a secondary emotion. Realizing this may help you reduce the amount of stress you experience. Suppose you're driving along and minding your own business when someone suddenly cuts you off. What's the first thing you feel? Anger? No! The first thing is fear: fear of losing your life, of having an accident, or of being out of control while driving your car. With the first thought of, I'm going to die, you have a shot of adrenaline. Your energy peaks.

In less time than it takes to snap your fingers, you see that you haven't died or had an accident and that your insurance rates aren't going up. The inner feeling of fear instantly becomes anger, which is turned outward. Now you may scream, curse, or make an obscene gesture to use up some of that adrenaline, as if the other person knew your pain or could hear you! Actually, fear is a powerful motivator and it explains a lot of human behavior. Whenever someone is angry, fear is fueling the anger. You can count on it. Fear is a primary emotion. Anger is a secondary emotion.

Crucializing

In an emergency we have to react; either we fight or take flight.

Although most situations aren't emergencies, many parents "crucialize" or see the less important details as being crucial. We blow things out of proportion, and our bodies pump adrenaline that we have no real need for. In some instances, parents become so hyper and distraught that they lose control.

In times of crucialization, a parent's paranoid fantasies take over. Paranoia is fear; a fantasy is make-believe. When someone you love is late or not where you expect them to be, have you ever imagined them bloody by the side of a road, in a hospital, kidnapped, or dead? Those are paranoid fantasies, and they can get the best of us. Think about it for a minute. Most of what we worry about doesn't come true anyway!

No one warned us that our soon-to-be-adopted-foster-son Robert was a runaway. Three months after he moved into our home at age 9, he was irritated about having to do chores and being teased by some boys at school. He walked into the house at 4:00 P.M. and out of the house at 5:00. At 11:30 P.M. we finally got a call that he was in the country, seven miles from where we lived, having milk and cookies provided by a compassionate new "friend." I understand about crucializing! Robert had no idea what we went through trying to find him. Once we did find him, I was furious. It took a long time for me to calm down from all of the paranoid fantasies that I had been entertaining in those six and a half hours. The next time Robert decided to "talk with his feet," as I came to call his disappearances, I stayed calmer.

A gem of parenting wisdom is appropriate here—instead of worrying so much about your children, put your energy to work by taking responsible action. We need to concentrate on "changing the things that we can" while letting go of the many things that are outside our control (including paranoid fantasies). I think that every parent should have the Serenity Prayer posted in an obvious place where they can read it every day:

THE SERENITY PRAYER

GOD GRANT ME
the SERENITY to accept
the things I cannot change.
The COURAGE to change
those that I can.
And the WISDOM
to know the difference.

—Reinhold Niebuhr

I soon came to realize that there was a lot about Robert and TJ that I would never know or understand, things I would have to accept. I learned to concentrate on changing the things that I could and let the rest go. I admit, though, that this lesson in life took me a long time before I was very effective with it.

Moving to Center

If you're unclear about what's the best way to proceed in a stressful situation, then you might establish a policy that's different from "Don't just stand there, do something." Wouldn't it be better to "Don't just do something, stand there?" Or, sit down in a "thinking chair" and figure out what's best to do. Take a "Wedge of Time." One of the most important reasons why this book was written is that I spent a lot of time thinking about my own family problems. Our family was in a stressful situation almost daily. I spent a lot of time thinking about each problem and the best thing to do about them.

You'll increase your ability to respond to a problem by getting in touch with your good thinking, love, and confidence (or R=TLC). This process can be called "moving to center" or to that place where your best decisions are made. You may want to talk things over with a good receptive listener—not someone who'll attempt to make your mind up for you by giving advice, but rather a person who'll let you air your ideas and feelings until you can come to your own conclusion about what the best action is. You know what to do. You just need time to figure it out. Remember: *Thinking Takes Time!*

In those situations when our worst fears are realized, worrying won't do much to prevent or change it. In fact, serenity for parents is contained in the following secret—the truth is that much that happens to our children isn't up to us. We as parents imagine that it is. We believe we're supposed to be bigger than life itself, but this kind of thinking only drives people crazy. The Serenity Prayer will help you sort out family problems and restore order to your mind.

Doom and Gloom

I've met parents that are stuck in how bad and awful it all is. "Poor me." According to them, life is one burden after another. They're forever victims. They're prisoners of their own mind. They're addicted to being negative. They live in chronic pessimism, and they can actually get very angry if you point out to them what they're doing. Because they focus only on pain, they live in perpetual fear. They haven't learned how to love. They don't live a Good Life, thus, all they know is stress.

The doom and gloom mentality is a disease that's epidemic in our society. Pick up the daily paper; listen to the news. Very little news is new. Much of it is old *bad* news! There are so many wonderfully courageous acts and beautiful things that happen to people every day, and we don't hear about them. They're not even considered news! You have to work really hard to stay positive with so much negativity around you. The truth is that no one can think a positive and a negative thought at the same time. In order for you to live a Good Life, you have to exercise discipline in what you pay attention to, to sort out and clean your thoughts by paying attention to what is positive. It also helps to keep toxic gloom-and-doom people at a distance. It isn't your job to save them or fix them. The only person you can "save" is yourself. Now let's see an example of positive coping and family crisis-handling in action.

The Wedge of Time

When Frances arrived home from a tough day at work, she saw Todd (11) and Jason (9) tearing around the house playing war games; the baby was filthy and screaming in her crib, the house was a shambles, and the new caregiver, Nina, was nowhere around. As Frances said later, she felt as if she'd had a blow to her gut. She was shaking all over. She didn't know whether to scream or cry.

Frances was in a reactive mode. She felt raw emotion. Rather than be a bull in a china shop, she called a new friend, Janet, who came over and calmed things down. Frances picked up the baby while Janet got Todd and Jason in line. An hour later, Nina came sauntering down the street and acted surprised that Frances was home so early. Frances fired her.

Janet was a true friend. She said, "Frances, if you go into your room and rest, I'll start dinner for you." Frances knew a gift when she saw it, and silently nodded her head. When she closed the door she felt weak in the knees. Her family was not working out. Something had to change. As soon as her head hit the pillow, she was out.

When she woke up two hours later at 7:00 P.M., she was in a panic. "Oh no. I've overslept!" She jumped out of bed and charged out the door to see what was wrong this time.

To her amazement, Todd and Jason were quietly washing dishes while Janet cleaned the stove. The baby was playing on a blanket and the house had been put back in order. Janet had lined up an emergency care-giver for the next day, and Frances's dinner was waiting for her on the table. Everything was so organized and calm.

What a difference in how Frances felt after resting compared to when she first came home three hours earlier. She experienced a Wedge of Time.

The Wedge of Time

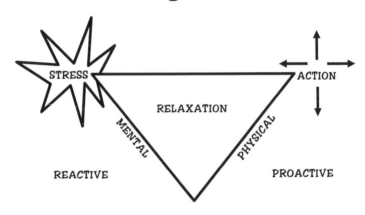

A Wedge of Time may be a few seconds (like counting from one to ten), five minutes, an hour, "I need to sleep on that tonight," days, weeks, or even months. Time helps us get a perspective on our problems. You decide how much time you need according to the needs of the situation.

The goal is to allow enough time to shift from the tension of stress to being relaxed. Our best thinking takes place when we feel relaxed and com-fortable, when we're coming from a loving place rather than a fearful one.

When you're in stress, your needs aren't being met, you feel frustrat-ed, and often your fear will turn to anger. At such a time, your thinking is *reactive*. Reactive thinking isn't clear. It's like the knee-jerk reaction when a doctor taps you on a nerve. You're likely to lash out and say or do the wrong thing. Give yourself a Wedge of Time so that you can choose an appropriate action instead of reacting inappropriately.

Thinking Takes Times

You'll have less stress when you're thinking straight. It's then that you start solving problems instead of making them. One of the best parenting secrets is The 3-T Rule, or "Thinking Takes Time." Most parents are not as efficient about time management as they need to be. They rush helter-skelter from one activity to another without allowing enough time for processing. Good thinking doesn't take a *lot* of time, but it does take *some* time. Consider it important and start to schedule it into your day.

THE 3-T RULE:
Thinking Takes Time

Successful families have time issues and daily routines figured out. With good organization, parents can make time to pursue their dreams and desires while being active parents. They make sacrifices, but they aren't self-sacrificial.

How much time do *you* need? It depends on your unique situation. Someone on the verge of a mental or physical breakdown may need a lot of time. Usually, a shorter time will do. A weekend away can do wonders. If a weekend vacation isn't possible, take a mini-vacation at home in a bubble bath with soft music and candlelight or spend time in a health club sauna. Go for a walk or, if you're more athletic, run around the block as fast as you can. Once you know how important this is, you'll find ways to include several Wedges of Time in even your busiest days. By taking a brief time to relax, you'll have a valuable tool to use whenever you feel your stress level escalating. And once you learn the relaxation response, it's easier to use these brief periods of time effectively.

The Relaxation Response

Being able to use your *relaxation response* is one of the most important tools you have for managing day-to-day stress. Actually, this response is something that you know how to do already. You do it every day, at least twice. You know how to go from being fully awake into sleep, and you know how to come out of sleep to being fully awake. The transition period from full awareness into your subconscious or sleep is called *twilight sleep.* You can go into twilight sleep without actually going to sleep. When you're asleep you're not aware of your surroundings, but in twilight sleep you're aware of where you are and what's going on—you just feel very relaxed about it.

When you enter twilight sleep, your blood pressure lowers, your brain waves slow down, and your thoughts drift. As you become more relaxed, you stop thinking about anything in particular. A good way to bring on the relaxation response is to count slowly from ten to one. As you mentally say "ten," breathe in and then slowly breathe out. As you exhale, feel some part of your body let go and relax. If you don't get this sensation, say the number again (and again) until you feel some part of your body release. Tell your body "I am relaxing" as you're counting.

Stay relaxed in twilight sleep until you feel rested. Your body tells you when you're rested, just as it does when you wake up after you've had enough sleep. You can go into a state of relaxation and take control of tension whenever you want to. Once you know how, you can successfully go into a resting state in less than five minutes. You can have the full benefit of a nap without taking the time a nap requires. You will enjoy practicing this skill until you can relax on command.

The relaxation response is an important part of understanding how to dance through the give-and-take of your life. We're so busy most of the time with our work and with our families that we forget that we need quiet time to let go and release negativity, clear our thoughts, and move into that center called love.

A key to good parenting is found in parents who are able to maintain control of their emotions. When you're "losing it" with your children, take time out; *don't take it out on them.* When experiencing maximum stress, you're of no use to anyone. Leave. Retreat. Change your attention to something positive. Learning to "relax on command" means learning to dance with grace. A parent who's able to do this with regularity has truly made a breakthrough.

I can hear you say, "What impractical advice. Who'll take care of my children while I pull myself together? How can I afford to take a vacation?" This is a problem to be carefully solved. If you're co-parenting, you and your partner can take turns. If you're a single parent, you'll survive with a network of friends like Janet, who also need to have private time. Many people trade child care to have more time to themselves. The parents I've seen who are in the worst shape are the rugged individualists who are trying to raise their children by themselves.

Understanding Change

If you understand the nature of change, you can learn to anticipate change and adapt to it without going crazy. Once someone told me, "All you can count on is change." Indeed, nothing has stayed the same. My children are grown, and many of the people I used to know have disappeared from my life. Our society bears little resemblance to the way it was when I was growing up. To be an exceptional parent, you have to be able to manage change and adapt to it by being flexible. Excessive stress over normal change can be damaging to you and to the whole family. These four stages of change can help you understand its natural cycles:

First, there is *breakdown*. Lifestyles we have come to treasure, relationships, corporations, social systems, and governments all feel the effect of change. In the breakdown period, there are power struggles to maintain the status quo, to make something fit that doesn't fit anymore. Our conclusions are challenged, and our illusions are burst. We tend to accept limiting ideas and be creatures of habit, and we are often more motivated by a fear of change. We see this when couples divorce; we have seen this in the breakdown of the USSR. We see it in our families as change continuously makes our circumstances different.

Second, there is *breakup*. This is the cycle where something gives and we reach a point of no turning back. Humpty Dumpty has fallen. This is a time to pick up the pieces, and to give up complaining and hanging on. This cycle of change is motivated by courage to let go and to face uncertainty.

Third, there is *breakout*. Here, people surrender the old way of thinking which is characterized by acceptance. In this cycle, you wouldn't go back if you could to previous conditions. People are motivated by curiosity and a realization that things could get better as change progresses.

Fourth, there is *breakthrough*. With an open mind, all sorts of possibilities come flooding through. This is the time of "Ah-ha!" and "Eureka!" Soon people settle into this stage and again subscribe to limiting ideas and become creatures of habit all over again. The cycle of change starts anew.

You can see how these four stages work by examining how Frances handled the fact that her family was not working. First, she saw the *breakdown* in the chaos caused by her childcare worker. Her family had been deteriorating into breakdown for some time. *Breakup* occurred when she fired Nina and became emotionally and physically exhausted. She moved into the *breakout* cycle when she saw how effectively Janet was able to handle a stressful situation. Finally, she reached *breakthrough* when she used the following six steps to solve her problems.

Problem Solving

An important part of the parenting process is to take the time you need to complete six steps for solving problems. Once you do, you'll find that you have fewer episodes of serious stress in your family. This will be to everyone's benefit. The six steps to problem solving are:

1. *What is the problem?*

2. *Analyze the problem.*

3. *What will solve the problem?*

4. *Make a plan.*

5. *Do it.*

6. *Evaluate.*

It's All Up to Me Syndrome

Many a parent is the victim of the "I have to do it all" syndrome. Frances decided not to be a victim when she called on Janet to help her. Then she took the following steps to get rid of the stress and prevent another crisis.

The Problem

"I'm doing too much. I have three children. I'm working a full-time job, then I go home and work another full-time job. I'm bone weary and feel that I'm sinking in quicksand. It's easier to do things myself than to hassle my children constantly to clean up after themselves."

Define the Problem

"This isn't fair. Our family needs to have the labor divided more fairly. Each person can learn to take care of his or her mess. Every child learns early to help clean up to the best of his or her ability. Good habits start young, and so do bad ones. I haven't delegated enough work around the house. Our new caregiver needs to be able to follow through in helping the children accept their share of the work load."

Solving the Problem

Frances said, "I learned to lay down the law and build on a concept of what's fair. I cited the Golden Rule of treating others the way you would like to be treated. No one wants to clean up after someone else's mess. So don't leave a mess. Each person is responsible for his or her own area, plus a portion of the common area."

The Plan

"Some chores are automatic. The boys are to clean up after they eat and keep their own area in the bedroom neat. The boys and I had several family meetings to decide on general household chores which were divided into A, B, and C lists. The A chores are the ones that are the hardest or that no one wants to do. The B chores are medium-hard, and the C chores aren't difficult to do. When all of the chores were listed, we decided how many of each chores would be assigned to each person. They all agreed to have the weekend chores done by Saturday noon."

Doing It

"It took a few months of supervision and attention to detail before everyone felt that the work load was fair. I used a lot of "catch them being good." They understood how appreciative I was for their cooperation. They refined the list so that the first pick for chores was rotated each week. On Saturday morning each person could play a half hour of music for everyone. When the children were younger, I planned an outing for them after Saturday chores. When they became teens, they were used to doing their share, bargaining, and picking the right time to get the job done. I included how to cook, how to shop for groceries, and how to pay household bills as they got older."

Evaluation

"Evaluating our family work delegation was a continuous process. As the children could take on more responsibility, I followed through to see that they were being successful. It took some time and organization for me to design and implement this plan, but once I got started I never felt like a victim again." She put these new tools in her parenting tool box: Thinking Takes Time and the Wedge of Time.

When I met Frances five years later she said, "The benefits to my family of insisting on a different way to share the load and be organized has been immeasurable. Each child learned a fair way to divide chores by using the art of negotiation. They all developed a strong sense of what's fair, and also what's an acceptable job. They learned to manage almost all of the household functions, including money management. They're responsible young people now. I'm proud of them."

Different Ways to Solve Family Problems

Here are some examples of parents solving their family problems in different ways. Note how each family chooses what's best for everyone based on its own unique situation.

A Career Path or a Mommy Path?

Frances' friend Janet was in a lucrative career, wore designer clothes, and had her hair and nails done weekly. After her two children arrived, she went back to the same high-paying job and was glad to do it. However, she reached a point where she saw that the benefits of the job were outweighed by the expenses of working and the cost of child care. She saw, too, that she was sacrificing a lot by being away from the children for so long.

After careful thought, she talked it over with her husband. Being a one-income family would mean living a much plainer lifestyle. They decided to postpone her career path for a mommy path for a few years. She found that she was equally content to be a stay-at-home wife and full-time nurturing mother. She made plans to resume her career when her children were older. She said, "I've had the best of the corporate world, now I want the best of family life. My children won't be young for long, and I don't want to feel that I missed out on their formative years." She used her time management and organizational skills to run her family efficiently. These are the same methods she demonstrated for Frances.

Less is More

Bob, a divorced father of three, stopped working over time to support an elegant lifestyle that he could rarely enjoy. He learned that less is more. "We clip coupons and plan menus on Wednesday. When we shop on Thursday, we buy quantities of fruit and vegetables in season. We can and freeze them. We rent videos and watch them together. I'm involved with my children's education. They get an allowance every week, out of which they must save something for their college. My children get a lot of strokes for being good students. I don't have trouble with any of them. I went from upper middle class to poor, but I'm richer than most people."

Saying No!

Patty said, "I had ulcers from trying to please everyone. I was in a constant panic, of rushing to keep up with all that I had to do. One day I asked myself, 'If I died tomorrow, what would all these people do? They would have to find someone else to do all the work for them or do it themselves.' It suddenly became very easy to say "No!" to family, friends, neighbors, organizations, and committees. I began to say "Yes!" to an afternoon nap, to exercising every morning, and going back to my relaxing hobbies. Everyone remarks about how much happier I am—and my ulcers are gone!"

Going Back to School

Jan went back to finish her teaching credentials. While her children were young, she was able to have a flexible schedule where she could enjoy the best of family life and take her time getting a college education. She paced her studies so she'd finish her degree about the time she'd feel comfortable leaving her children to become a full-time teacher.

Ending Worry and Guilt

Annette told me that after her oldest boy, Bucky, got a small motorcycle, she worried incessantly when he was out on it. He wasn't careless. He understood all the safety precautions. He was on the honor role at school. Still, she couldn't sleep until she knew he was home.

As she was fretting one evening, she got the dreaded call. Bucky had been killed. It wasn't his fault. He was waiting at a corner for a light to turn when a car slammed into him.

After the funeral, she had a great insight. None of her worrying had kept Bucky alive. She was not in a position to protect him when he was in danger. He was no longer a little child. She vowed to do all she could to teach her two youngest children to be responsible, and to let go of worry forever. "It will be the way it will be," she said. And she told us that she never worried about her children again.

Letting Go

Worry is a lot like "guilt"—neither can make things better. What does make things better is to solve family problems to the best of your ability and then let them go. Recite the Serenity Prayer.

Reduce stress in your life with this parenting secret—you'll find family living a lot more enjoyable if you decide to give every day your best effort and accept that there are limits to what you can do. Don't hold any illusions about having to be perfect. Admit it when you've made a mistake, and grow from the experience. Be prepared to be tolerant of other people's judgments that you "aren't good enough." Consider the source and focus on your successes. That's where your strength is. Learn to enjoy the journey!

Parenting, and raising a family, isn't all up to you. You're part of a team. If you work to the best of your ability, then that's all you can do. It's enough. If you hold that same sentiment for your children, spouse, relatives and friends, you will be well loved.

When times are tough or when you're in a crisis, the Serenity Prayer can bring you peace of mind as you sort through what you can change and what you'll have to accept. Remember, the word *accept* doesn't mean that you have to like it. When I accept something, it means that this situation is not in my control, and I release it with no further worry or guilt.

Will your children turn out to be as smart, clever, successful, charming, and appreciative as you thought? Probably not. Parents have a hard time accepting that they don't control all the influences on their children. Our children are individuals with independent minds and preferences. As our children grow older, parents must step back and watch them choose according to what feels right for them, not for us. Will they make mistakes? Sure, this is how they'll learn. They have a right to pursue their happiness, even if their definition is different from your own.

Sometimes it helps to remind people of the obvious: birth certificates don't come with guarantees. Relax into your parenting responsibilities. You wouldn't be reading this book if you weren't a responsible person. Take time right now to congratulate yourself on taking this opportunity to grow.

♥

CHAPTER NINE

COMMUNICATING ASSERTIVELY

We communicate our thoughts and feelings with our eyes and our bodies as well as with our words. We cannot avoid communicating. What we communicate to our children, however, is not always the message we hope to get across. In this chapter, you'll learn how to get your ideas across assertively. No parenting skill is more important than communicating with an assertive voice.

The Nature of Emotions

There are two primary emotions: *love* and *fear*. All of the other emotions are secondary emotions, variations of these two themes. At any given time, you are either feeling love or you are feeling fear. The only way to overcome fear is to overcome it with love. Some parents fear the loss of love so much that they lose sight of their own needs, and the Good Life that they deserve.

You can't communicate assertively unless you understand how our emotions work. It's our nature to feel, to be emotional, and to have mood changes. Feelings are ever-present. They're with us even when we sleep, and if we feel anxious and upset, we may have nightmares. Telling people not to be emotional is to go against their very nature. The majority of communication is done with our tone of voice and body language, which reflect our emotions more than words.

Our Birthright

Because feelings are our birthright, it's essential to recognize them in ourselves, in our children and in others, and to learn to express a wide range of emotions. We can tell a lot about what people are feeling by watching their eyes. We can also read their emotions by observing body language. The heart of communication requires understanding the nuances of how love and fear interact with each other. A good communicator knows that people's feelings are essential to understanding the total picture. Notice how many times you can tell if someone is happy or sad, angry or comfortable—just by observation alone.

Feelings are also transitory. Just because you're angry now, doesn't mean that you'll still be angry in five minutes. Even grief subsides, and a child who has experienced grief over the loss of a pet can quickly become ecstatic over the idea of a trip to an amusement park, and then move back into sadness over the loss of the pet again. Moods have an ebb and flow, changing according to circumstances.

Acting from Emotions

By themselves, feelings are neither right nor wrong. Your feelings are personal; they're the way you experience your world. There's always a reason for what you're feeling. In most instances it's more beneficial to acknowledge what you're feeling and why you feel the way you do than it is to keep your feelings hidden.

Having certain feelings, of course, doesn't mean that you're entitled to act on them. For example: I can feel murder in my heart, but I don't have a right to kill someone. There's a big difference between what you're entitled to feel and having a right to take action.

The Golden Rule, "Treat people the way you would like to be treated," and the Universal Rule, "Act the way you would want everyone to act," are used in cultures around the world to guide decision making about what behavior is right or wrong. Most parents will say, "How would you like it if someone treated you that way?" or "What if everyone did that?" What if everyone lied, cheated or stole from people, or took action on every emotion they experienced?

The Golden Rule:
Would you like to be treated that way?

The Universal Rule:
What if everybody did it?

Suppose Sam feels angry towards his newborn sister, Susan. Sam has his private logic for feeling that way. Simply saying, "No, you shouldn't feel that way," isn't going to easily change Sam's feelings or correct the situation. Sam has a right not to like his little sister, but he doesn't have a right to hurt her. Sam can't change the fact that his sister was born and now requires considerable time with her parents. No longer the only child who receives most of the attention, he has to share his parents—and it doesn't feel good. Like many other first-born children, he'll change how he feels about his sister. With good parental help, he can still feel important. He can get approval for helping and learn to look forward to playing with his sister in the future. His parents can also arrange to be alone with Sam from time to time as he grows used to having his sister around.

Trust your intuitions! No one can take care of children for very long without being exposed to a wide range of emotional states. Both boys and girls need to learn compassion and empathy. There's no more important way to learn these emotions than for parents to demonstrate compassion by being receptive and by giving children permission to express their feelings. If you "catch them" at expressing their true feelings, and tell them that this is valuable to do, they'll be more likely to express themselves in other situations.

You don't have to *like* it when a child says, "I hate you!" and other unpleasantries. A simple acknowledgment of their feelings is enough. "I understand that you're really mad at me right now." You can use a Wedge of Time and solve this problem later, and that's sufficient as long as you've provided a safe environment to let them talk.

In the family, it's critical that every child learn cooperation, teamwork, and mutual help. Competing has its place, but that's on the playing field. Learning to compete is important, but not at the exclusion of cooperation. Young boys and girls must learn how to manage their emotions in nondestructive ways. This will make them strong and responsible individuals as adults. Effective communicators are clear about what they're feeling, and they're also comfortable expressing their feelings.

Do you want your children to tell you the truth? Of course, you do. Yet, many parents slam the door in a child's face when they're telling the truth. You don't always "want" to hear it, but you realize that you're better off for hearing the truth. The importance of teaching children to express their feelings is equal to the importance of teaching them to tell the truth. What we feel *is* true. It may not be true five minutes from now. The "I hate you!" often turns into "I'm sorry, Mommy. I love you!" Remember that children think in the immediate, and they don't realize how to be subtle. I'm not suggesting that children be given license to say cruel things to people whenever they feel like it. All children need to be taught how to express themselves appropriately. They can't be responsible until they do. It takes countless experiences to learn this skill.

The Moral Emotions

In order for us to do an effective job of listening receptively to our children and others, we need to recreate the other person's feelings based on what we ourselves have experienced in our past. For example, if Sammy has never experienced grief, he wouldn't know how a grieving person feels. Also, if Sally has never experienced joy, she wouldn't know what joyous people are feeling. *Sympathy* and *empathy* are the moral emotions. These are the feelings that enable us to understand what another person is feeling.

Empathy is to feel *with* another person. Suppose Fred's Uncle Jack meets a tragic death. His family and friends gather together for the funeral. Everybody is feeling grief at the same time. That's empathy, to feel with another person.

Sympathy is to feel *for* another person. Mike worked in the same company as Jack. Mike had a similar experience when a relative came to a tragic end. He felt sympathy for the situation. He felt for the people who were grieving, but wasn't actually participating in the grief process at that time.

These two emotional states, empathy and sympathy, require the ability to conceptualize mentally what another person is feeling. The only way you can do this is by listening receptively to the other person and then drawing upon your own experiences.

Empathy and sympathy are abstract thoughts. Abstractions are ideas that you can't touch. No one has ever touched truth, beauty, justice or love, yet we have all experienced thinking about these things.

Young children experience their world literally. Life is full of contrasts for them. They understand "Yes" and "No"; they don't understand "Maybe." It takes many experiences and more developed thinking processes before they're capable of the abstract thought that empathy and sympathy require. You'll use empathy and sympathy when you receptively listen to your children and communicate effectively with them, always encouraging them to express their feelings and be truthful.

Receptive Listening

There are two sides of good communication, and one of them is receptive listening. Receptive listening involves doing three things at once: determine what the other person is feeling, about what, and why. We recreate the other person's feelings by using empathy and sympathy.

You are _____ **,**
            (feeling)

about _____ **,**
          (what)

_____
        (why)

Receptive listening entails listening carefully to the words the other person says, looking the person in the eye, and observing his or her body language. It also means avoiding questions, at least in the beginning, and using "door openers." Door openers are verbal and non-verbal cues that you're listening by nodding your head or saying "uh-huh." Finally, check to see if you understand what you're being told by telling the person what you think you just heard—putting it into your own words. (These stages of receptive listening may differ somewhat in various cultural groups. Good receptive listening is always culturally-appropriate.)

One night at The Parent Connection, Terry asked me, "How do you ignore a nine-month-old baby?" Her words were less important than her looks and the tone of her voice. She had puffy red eyes, her clothes were mismatched, she slouched over, and her voice was flat. I received what she was telling me without questioning her, and I didn't discount what she was saying by telling her, "You shouldn't feel that way." The situation was critical. She needed to be heard! Instead, I made a statement, "You look like you're having a rough time." This was enough to open the flood gates and to let the real issues come flowing out.

You're not listening receptively if you cut off the person who's expressing his or her feelings, or if you assume that you must solve that person's problem rather than allowing him or her to come to their own conclusions. Don't expect that the problem will be solved on the spot. Listening may be more important than offering a solution. Also, you have to know what the problem is before you can be helpful. Receptive listening may take two seconds, a few minutes, or several hours.

If you're not able to listen receptively when someone calls upon you, say so and ask for another time. If you're at a low point where you yourself need to be listened to, don't take on someone else's problems. Avoid saying, "I know how you feel." No one knows how another person really feels because we all have unique experiences.

The Tip of the Iceberg

It isn't safe to be overly trusting with strangers, and most people have to build trust before they can express to others what's really going on inside of them. As you know, only about 1/9 of an iceberg floats above water. This is also as much as people are willing to show of themselves. The public self is how we look, what we say, and how we act when we don't know the other person well. The other 8/9 are our private selves which exist below the surface. We expose our private selves after developing trust. One of the ways that trust develops between parents and children is when they receptively listen to each other. Good listeners build trust, creating an atmosphere where children feel safe to be open about their problems, feelings, and concerns. Who will children talk to about their fears, desires and dreams, if not you? Receptive listening is a skill you need so that you can listen to your children's private concerns without getting angry, judging, or putting them down.

"I" Statements

An "I" Statement is the other side of receiving: it's giving information to the person you're communicating with. "I" statements are assertive ways of expressing your feelings honestly and clearly so that the other person will understand. In problem solving, this technique demonstrates that you "own" the primary problem, and you're taking responsibility for solving your problem.

I am _____ ,
(feeling)

about _____ ,
(what)

_____
(why)

"I" Statements do three things at once: express my feelings, clarify what I'm talking about, and explain why. "I" Statements can involve a great variety of positive and negative feelings. They may range from feelings of love to feelings of hate. The "I" Statement keeps ownership of your problem with you rather than blaming someone else or debating who is right.

"I'm feeling frustrated by having to wait, when we agreed to leave by 5:00 P.M."

"This music is irritating to me. I want to be able to concentrate on my work."

"I love the way everyone helped out when I wasn't feeling well."

Avoiding the Accusatory You

An "I" Statement is best received by the listener when it is non-critical. The secret is to avoid the "accusatory you," that is, blaming the other person or being critical. Most people shut down when they hear it. We can express almost any feeling when we keep ownership of the problem with ourselves. We have a right to feel the way we do. It's no one else's fault if we're mad, sad, frustrated, or disappointed. Sound mental health entails claiming ownership of our feelings without blaming others for "making" us feel a certain way. You can see the difference in these examples:

"You forgot to lock the door and the dog got out." vs.
    "The door was left open and the dog got out."

"I don't like it when you interrupt me." vs.
    "I don't like it when I'm interrupted."

We shut down when we hear the word "you" used as a weapon of blame.

Tips on Using "I" Statements

When you make an assertive "I" Statement to a child or family member, look the person in the eye and use body language. Include the three parts of the formula: feeling, about what, and why. Here are some other good communication secrets:

- Be aware that the person you talk to might have to think about your requests. (Thinking takes time.)
- Ask for another time if the person isn't hearing you now.
- Truth is your friend. "I" Statements are convincing and are hard to argue with. Thus, they help prevent an argument or power struggle.
- "I" Statements are a plea for help—most people like to feel like they're being helpful.
- If you have something important to say, you have an obligation to say it in a way that it can be received.
- Ask for what you want. (Many people don't live the Good Life and take care of their needs simply because they don't know how to ask for what they want.)
- Show respect for the person you're communicating with, especially for your children. Avoid attacking the person. Instead, describe the exact behavior (without the accusatory "you") that's bothering you.

"I" Statements provide a valuable way for others to know the limits of what you'll accept. Don't embrace the myth that you should avoid the truth about how you feel because it might hurt someone. People need to know the truth in order to make rational choices. "I" Statements are a way to tell the truth in a nonattacking way. They're a very effective way to communicate.

Kinds of Sentences

The *kind* of sentences you use makes a big difference in how effectively you communicate.

Commands

Typically, parents issue these commands to their children each morning.

"Get up."	"Get dressed."
"Wash your face."	"Brush your teeth."
"Make your bed."	"Eat your breakfast."
"Hurry up."	"Let's go."

Does that sound familiar? Some parents say they've thought of putting this litany on a tape recorder because they're tired of saying it over and over. Parents sigh, "Why is it necessary to do this? Why don't my children ever learn?"

Commands are orders. "Do this." "Don't do that." Orders demand that certain behaviors be performed, no questions asked. Sergeants bark out commands to their new recruits. The recruits are supposed to obey the commands without question. This military model is followed in many homes where commands are the chief form of communication from parent to child.

"Stop fighting."	"Clean your room."
"Shut up."	"Don't talk with your mouth full."

Commands don't work very well in a home setting. First, they encourage passivity. Children who are used to being talked to by commands rapidly learn that they don't have to think for themselves. All they have to do is wait and someone will tell them what to do next. What's more, excessive commands diminish a child's initiative to think about what to do next. Commands also can undermine confidence. "Sit down." "Be quiet." Do your work." Children realize, "I don't have to think for myself." Commands don't teach self-discipline.

Second, commands can be aggressive ways of speaking *at* children, not *with* them. They attempt to take away a child's freedom of choice. To disobey a command is to say "let's fight." Commands invite power struggles. When parents are feeling angry or stressful, they're quick to resort to expressing sharp commands. In fact, most people don't talk to each other in such a harsh way. It shows a lack of respect. Giving adults commands makes them feel that they're *being treated like children,* and it makes children feel that they're being talked down to.

Another parenting secret—communication is effective when we express our feelings in ways that get us the results we want; at the same time, it's important to be receptive to the feelings of your children. Aggressive feelings are usually expressed in an irritated or hostile way. They're then received with pain of one kind or another. The child you addressed may feel hurt, angry, unloved, or put down. Most commands are more aggressive than assertive.

Questions

My experience in teaching assertiveness for parents is that most people are unaware that *how* they're addressing a problem *is* the problem! We tend to feel safe asking questions without realizing that the questions lead us to trouble. We need to ask our children questions to get information, but using questions to try to get things done can perpetuate conflict. In this instance, questions seem to put the burden of decision on the child. Some questions can be manipulative, too, in that the answer you want is clearly implied though not directly stated. Notice how these questions will lead to power contests with children:

> "Why don't you put the dishes away?"
> "Don't you think the music is too loud?"
> "Isn't it time for you to go to bed?"
> "Wouldn't it be nice if you picked up toys now?"
> "Can't you play somewhere else?"

Say the sentences out loud, only this time use that irritated voice you get when you're frustrated. Visualize how the combination of questioning and being irritated give a lopsided amount of power to the child. The child can answer:

> "I don't know."
> "No."
> "I'm not sleepy."
> "I'll do it later."
> "Yeah," and then they'll do nothing.

An irritated voice only makes children dig in their heels and become less cooperative. Power plays don't get the job done. Many parents lead with a question in order to deflect attention from themselves or to sound more polite. It can be a delicate or soft way of attempting to get cooperation. And, of course, sometimes it works. However, by leading with a question, you're giving up your power to the child, rather than sharing power by encouraging participation. You may have noticed that children often don't respond to the soft sell.

> Mom: Jenny, isn't it your turn to do the dishes?
> Jenny: I don't know. I thought I did them last night.
> Mom: Don't you think the kitchen is a mess and that it would look better cleaned up?
> Jenny: Probably.
> Mom: Why don't you get into the kitchen and get the dishes cleaned up now?

Jenny: Oh, okay.

Mom: (One hour later) Jenny, why haven't you done the dishes?

Jenny: In a minute. (Mom looks exasperated. Two hours later, Jenny is getting ready for bed.)

Mom: Jenny, why can't you do your share of helping around the house? Now it's too late and I've got to do the dishes. (Mother stomps off into the kitchen and does the dishes as Jenny quietly goes to bed.)

Can you see how Mom's questioning gives Jenny power? In fact, so much power she can artfully stall until she doesn't have any work to do. Mom is not being assertive with Jenny.

Statement Sentences

Statements are assertive because they inform. They express facts. Without statement sentences you wouldn't know what's true. Truth is a parent's friend and best ally. Truth can stop an argument. Have you ever tried to argue with the truth? Even little children don't argue with the truth, at least not for long.

All houses get dirty, and so do cars. Everyone needs to sleep, eat, and have quiet time. Truth gives a context for understanding reality. Truth is the heart and soul of rational thought, the essence of good thinking. When you have to make an important decision, do you want to rely on all the facts you can get? Or do you want to decide according to partial truth or outright lies? The problem with lies is that they're intended to mislead, to distort the truth. They get in the way of making good decisions. Responsible people want to know the truth. No one can function at R=TLC without the accurate information that statement sentences provide.

At The Parent Connection, I've seen thousands of parents dramatically reach a breakthrough in the way that they communicate with their children. By training themselves to be assertive, parents can rely on statements to give their children information, avoiding unnecessary questions and commands.

Here are some examples of weak sentences:

(Command) "Clean your room." / "I'll do it later."
(Question) "Why don't you clean your room?" / "I don't want to."

Here are the steps Mom takes with Jenny to communicate assertively:

Step One: "Your room has gotten very dirty and disorganized. It's your job to keep it presentable."

Step Two: "You're to have your room cleaned by dinner tonight. Dinner is at 6 P.M."

Statements require more words, but not so many words that it's hard to understand. Use just enough words to describe the situation, set the limit, and tell when.

Step Three: *Follow through (when the child completed the task).* "You did a terrific job of cleaning your room. I can see that you've dusted, vacuumed, taken the trash out and—my goodness—even your desk is organized. I'll bet that you'll enjoy it a lot more that way."

Notice that by specifically describing what was done, the correct behavior is strengthened. This helps children continually build their sense of knowing. It requires many experiences to attain a state of knowing.

Follow through (when the child partially completed the task). "You've dusted and cleaned up your desk. (catch them being good) When the trash is out and you've vacuumed, you'll be finished. This needs to be done now so that you'll be ready for dinner on time."

Follow through (when the child didn't accomplish the task). "I don't see that any work has been done toward cleaning your room. We have a serious disagreement here. If you're having a problem that I don't know about, then we should talk about it now." (Problem Solving)

"I just didn't feel like doing it."

"This wasn't a good time for you. I need to know when you expect to have your room clean." (Participation in Solving the Problem.)

"By tonight."

"At what time?"

"By 7:30. I want to watch TV then."

"Fine. I'd like you to let me know when you're finished. In the meantime, if you get a phone call, I'll let the person know that you'll not be able to talk until you're finished cleaning your room." (Grandma's Rule)

Statement sentences are the work horses of communication, and they're one of the finest secrets of good parenting. They have power because they're direct, use facts, and don't invite power struggles. They're a respectful and mature way of expressing yourself. With practice, you'll learn to rely on them and when you use them, you'll immediately be more effective as a parent. In fact, you'll also be a more effective communicator.

Practice with Kinds of Sentences

Study the effectiveness of these sentences. Can you see how using a few more words results in better understanding?

> (Command) "Be quiet."
> (Question) "Why don't you be quiet?"
> (Statement) "I have a headache and I need you to be quiet. After I rest for an hour, we can play a game."

> (Command) "Sit down."
> (Question) "Don't you want to sit down?"
> (Statement) "When you sit down we'll begin the video. The rest of us are waiting for you."

> (Command) "Go to bed."
> (Question) "Will you go to bed?"
> (Statement) "It's 8:00 P.M. and time to go to bed. I'll read you a story when you're in bed."

> (Command) "Don't do that."
> (Question) "Aren't you going to stop that?"
> (Statement) "A dog's tail isn't meant to be pulled. When you pull the dog's tail, it hurts him."

> (Command) "Get ready."
> (Question) "Are you ready to go?"
> (Statement) "We're going to be late if we don't go now. We want to be on time for the movie."

Which to Be: Assertive, Passive, or Aggressive?

To be *assertive* means to declare your feelings directly and clearly about a situation, and to provide information that explains why you feel that way. Being assertive is to act in your best interests by speaking up for yourself. Assertive people express their feelings honestly and comfortably. They exercise their personal rights without denying the rights of others.

Being *passive* means being apathetic, uninvolved, and not speaking up when you should. Passive people rely a lot on questions. Questions deflect attention "from me to you." Being passive isn't always bad, however. It can also mean retreating from involvement in order to observe what's going on by using receptive listening. This means being keenly tuned into what's said and done. It entails heightening your senses of comprehension and understanding what's taking place. However, your goal as a parent is to do something about a problem with your children, not to just let it slide by.

To be *aggressive* means to use intimidation, fear or force as a way of controlling, sometimes causing physical or psychological damage. Aggressive behavior has no place in responsible parenting, and only encourages aggressive behavior on the part of children. Children deserve to be treated with dignity and respect. Aggression sabotages the goal of R=TLC.

"I Don't Know"

Have you ever tried to have a meaningful discussion with a child stuck in "I don't know"? There's nothing more maddening than an endless repetition of "I don't know" to whatever you ask. The way to get past this obstacle assertively is to lean forward slightly, look the child in the eyes expectantly, and with conviction say, "'I don't know' is not an answer." Then wait. If this doesn't bring an immediately response, say, "If you need time to think about it, we can talk in a few minutes." Then, consistently follow through! You'll be happy that you broke this bad habit.

The Dance of Life

In the chapter on stress management, we saw that all human beings experience a "fight or flight" response when in danger. Even when we experience normal stress and are not in real danger, we still react according to this natural response. We aren't the only living things to respond this way; animals, too, have the "fight or flight" response.

Monte Roberts, the horse trainer we met earlier, has become world famous because he understands this phenomenon very well. He's developed a remarkable way of taming wild horses. To "break" a horse can take more than three weeks of hard work. Some trainers use painful bits, spurs, and whips to force a horse into submission. The result is that the now-tame horse is afraid of not minding people.

Monte thinks that fear causes damage to the horse's spirit, which is akin to self-esteem in humans. He never "breaks" a horse. Instead, he "starts" or "joins up" with the horse.

As a small boy, Monte had countless opportunities to study horses. He was interested in what made them run at one time, and stand still at others. He found that he could enter a ring with a wild horse and "join up" very quickly. He replaced fear with trust, and soon bonded with the horse.

I first heard about Monte Roberts in a *Los Angeles Times* article. The headline "Educators Observe Horse Trainer for Ideas to Teach Children" caught my eye. What does Monte's technique have to do with people? Can it work as a method for training children—especially children who are wild? What is his technique? I was determined to meet him and to see a demonstration. I wasn't disappointed. In twenty-five minutes, Monte had tamed a wild horse. I was fascinated.

What is there about Monte's technique that can be used with people? Plenty! The technique is based on the concept of advance/retreat. Animals and people give off cues as to when they can be approached, and when to stay away. When the light is green, move forward; when the light is yellow, use caution; when the light is red, stop. Monte is extending the technique of receptive listening to reading body language as he determines what color the light is.

Put into practice, the concept of advance/retreat is the art of negotiation, selling, and teaching. I think of it as loving elevated to an art form. It is the *best* demonstration of receptive listening I've seen, and great for successful parenting. It's tricky knowing when to advance and when to retreat with your children. It means being sensitive to their feelings, words, and body language that signal what to do next. It isn't necessary to ask questions when you have the "feel" of the technique, any more than Monte would ask a horse, "Do you want to be friends yet?" He knows what the horse is thinking by observation alone.

THE DANCE OF LIFE:

Fight or Flight
Advance or Retreat
Approach or Pull Back

Over 80% of communication is through body language and tone of voice, not with words. You can establish trust between you and your children with tender loving care, not whips, belts, paddles, and harsh words that build fear. Sophisticated parents can read a child's signals of when to move forward and when to pull back or stop. They decide which of the four leadership styles to use according to the needs of the situation: take charge, benevolent, democratic, or hands off. Watch your child's body language, listen to the tone of voice, and read the gestures. Be conscious, too, of your own nonverbal messages, and see that they don't contradict what you're saying.

For example, if you touched your child's hair and she frowned and pulled away, would you continue attempting to stroke her hair? On the other hand, if she smiled and snuggled up to you, you'd realize that you were being given a response that indicates she wants more affection.

To summarize this key parenting secret, you can use the idea of advance/retreat to discipline, not to punish, your child and keep his or her self-esteem and confidence intact. The rewards are well worth the effort. With practice, your ability to communicate will take on a new dimension of effectiveness. You'll be moving exquisitely to the Dance of Life, and will be one of the few parents who have reached a breakthrough in the ability to communicate with this degree of sophistication. Your children will be truly blessed.

❤

CHAPTER TEN

DISCIPLINE WITH LOVE

What is Discipline?

It's helpful to first define what I mean by "disciplining with love." According to Webster's Dictionary, *discipline* means:

- Instruction and exercise designed to train proper conduct or action; and
- To learn a set or system of rules and regulations.

Discipline means "to teach." *Discipline with love* means to teach right from wrong using tender loving care. It doesn't mean punishment, that is, using physical or psychological force to control. Many people use the words discipline and punishment interchangeably. For the purposes of this book, *punishment* is intended to mean causing another pain or suffering, either mentally or physically. Discipline with love relies more on influence and rewards rather than on raw power to accomplish the goal of training children to be responsible. A disciplined child understands the difference between free choice and necessary boundaries.

Three Proven Steps to Discipline With Love

I'm excited to share with you The Parent Connection's tried-and-true

Three Steps to disciplining with love. These steps are essential to successfully teaching children and enabling them to reach their potential. As you practice the Three Steps, you'll find your children beginning to take charge of their lives. Once you know the Steps, you can use them over and over to build a better relationship with your children—and they'll always be grateful that you did.

Step I: Teach Right From Wrong

This three-step method develops a child's ability to be responsible by encouraging good thinking in word and deed. As we've already noted, children are great mimics. The way parents teach most is by example. Many parents are amazed to find that young children don't understand many of the words we say. Why? We talk too much. Children have short attention spans, and we use words and concepts they don't know. Children are far more interested in what we *do* than in what we *say*.

Teaching children right from wrong requires continuous diligence from parents. Have you ever noticed how you can "steer" your child along? Ricky, for example, strays off course by playing too rough and Mom corrects his behavior. Lucy has a sweet tooth that isn't good for her, and Dad tells her "No," and he hands her an apple.

This steering mechanism that parents use is subtle and constant. Chelsea (5) has managed to knock over her milk three days in a row. Pat uses Step I to teach her a lesson that one year from now she'll not remember ever having learned.

"Chelsea, the spilt milk makes an awful mess and interrupts dinner. If you leave your glass at the top of your plate, you'll be less likely to knock it over."

Step I is the answer to the question of *why we do what we do*. Your goal is helping your child develop the ability to think straight. Use words she understands. Check to make sure she has understood the reason why.

When Will You Be Quiet?

One mistake many parents make is explaining too much. Your parenting job is to explain only as much as your child is able to understand. Make the explanation appropriate to your child's age.

Sherryl (12) has become a TV addict. She watches over seven hours of TV a day. Wanda has been realizing that she needs to do something about it.

Just home after a stressful and exhausting day, she's annoyed to see Sherryl glued to the TV again. Sherryl doesn't even acknowledge her mother's coming through the door. Wanda lectures her on the importance of doing other things besides watching TV. TV won't help her get an education, be successful in life, exercise, and socialize. She should be a good girl so she'll have a bright future, etc., etc., etc. After a long dissertation on the horrors of too much TV, Wanda asks Sherryl, "Now, do you understand?" Sherryl nods her head, "Yes."

Children are smart enough to nod "Yes" just to end a parent's monologue. But usually, children only understand a tiny fraction of what their parents say, mostly because parents lecture instead of using a conversational approach. Children find lectures unpleasant and tune them out.

Is the Timing Right?

To maximize your results, pick a time when your child is willing to listen to you. Also, pick a time when you can get your point across clearly and calmly without losing your temper.

When Wanda walked through the door and saw Sherryl watching TV, it sparked her anger. This added to her problems. She'd had a tough day at work. Her first reaction was to lecture Sherryl.

After learning stress-management skills, Wanda realized that if she chose this particular moment to address Sherryl's TV problem, the timing would be off. She needed to unwind and rest first.

Wanda might look at Sherryl face to face and say, "Sherryl, I'm worried that you're watching too much TV. You watch at least seven hours of TV a day. That is way too much. We are going to make a plan for you to do more than watch TV. The TV will be turned off until we decide on a plan. We'll talk about it after dinner. I need to rest now."

Sherryl and Wanda wrote out a contract. Sherryl made a plan for seven hours of TV a week, not seven hours a day. She carefully chose programs she wanted to watch. She logged her TV time. She also started going to after-school sports, talked to her friends on the phone, read some new books, and went skating once a week. Her grades improved at school when she had enough time for her homework.

In other situations, the timing for discipline should be immediate. If you wait until after dinner before telling a small child that he shouldn't play with matches, he may not understand what you mean or remember what he did. When setting *safety* limits and there is pending danger, the timing must be immediate—always.

Does Chris Want to Be Scalded?

Another mistake parents often make is to use words and concepts a child cannot understand. The explanation needs to be age-appropriate.

Chris (6) plays with his truck next to the kitchen stove. Pots are bubbling as Judy busily cooks dinner. Judy says, "Chris, don't play by the stove. A pot could fall on you and you could be scalded." Chris drives his truck near the refrigerator, which is safely out of the way. Five minutes later, he's back next to the stove.

Would you conclude from Chris' actions that he wants to get scalded? What's really wrong here? Six-year-olds don't know what "scalded" means. In fact, children don't understand many of the "big" words grown-ups use.

One of the first concepts most parents teach their children is "hot." The word "hot" can stand for many things, and we want our children to learn early in life not to touch hot things. Art tells Danny, "The coffee cup is hot. The stove is hot. The iron is hot. The fireplace is hot." Then the parent hands Danny a bottle of hot sauce, and says how "hot" it is. None of the other categories of "hot" fit this one. There's so much to learn! Young children have difficulty differentiating from one situation to another. Children need careful teaching in each instance of "hot" so they can develop a concept of "hot" that has multiple meanings. Just think of how many concepts you've learned and how long it took you to learn them! It's no wonder that one of the finer qualities of successful parents is patience. When you understand how children think, it's easier to be patient.

The Easy Way

There is one very easy technique, used over and over again, that builds discipline, strengthens love, and prevents problems from occurring. It deserves repeating because it is one of the most important breakthrough parenting techniques of the twentieth century. It's called "Catch Them Being Good." Think of all the opportunities your children present to you daily where you can give them a pat on the back or an enthusiastic thank you. "You did it! Good for you!" "I love you!" Showing approval and providing acknowledgment for success motivates all of us. Everyone wants more pleasure than pain. Let's see how we can diminish pain by focusing on what's good.

Parents who have difficulty with this technique were usually raised under the "Catch Them Being *Bad*" method. Their own self-esteem has been so undermined that they only notice mistakes. It may take determination to give yourself praise for a job well done. "Catch Them Being Good" is the most important way to build R=TLC that I know of.

Receptive Listening—the Skill that Makes a Big Difference

"A good listener is not only popular everywhere, but after awhile he knows something."
                                                              —Jackie Mason, comedian

Your ability to be successful using Step I is directly related to your ability to listen receptively. What you want to know is whether you're being heard. Since children know how to look you in the eye and nod "yes" when their minds are elsewhere, you can best determine if you've been heard by watching their body language and asking for feedback. Avoid lecturing, or communication without participation. Instead, use conversation. When your children dialogue with you, they'll be far more likely to listen. If you're still meeting resistance, wait for a better time. Children change their minds quickly, so you probably won't have to wait long.

In the first step, you've been busy teaching your child *why* you want their behavior to change. Though children may not be mature enough to understand all the reasons, as they grow older they'll deepen their understanding of what you've been teaching them. Once parents have done the explaining in Step I, the next step is to set limits, simply and clearly. Let's go to Step II.

➡ Step II: Setting Limits

Step I: Teach Right From Wrong

Step II is Setting Limits, and there are three essential parts to setting limits, known as "The 3 Ws." The 3 Ws are Who, What, and When. The answer to "Who" is "You." I emphasize this point because too many parents dilute their statement by saying, "I want you to...." The "I want" introduces an element of "Do it to *please* me." A power-hungry child might interpret this as a way to get around the limit, thinking, "I don't care what you want; *I* want to do as I please."

Instead, use an assertive statement that starts with "you." "You are to...." Next, explain "What" is to be done: "clean up the spilt milk." Finally, be specific about when it's to be done. "When?" "Now," or some other time frame that's appropriate to the situation.

Many parents fail at setting limits because they don't specify the essential "when." A child's sense of time is quite different from ours. When you say "now," it means immediately. If you said, "As soon as you can," your child may think you mean "by dinnertime, before bedtime, after the TV show, next week" or "I'll just wait and see what happens." The sentence in our example which sets the limits reads, "You are to clean up the spilt milk now."

The 3 Ws:

You	are to clean up the spilt milk	now.
↓	↓	↓
Who	**What**	**When**

(a) Mandatory Limits

Just as there are three steps to setting limits, there are also three different kinds of limits. First are *mandatory limits*. Mandatory means you must obey because of the importance of the situation. Safety rules are mandatory because they can mean life or death. It's mandatory that Terry learn to not turn the knobs on the gas range until he's old enough to understand how to use the stove safely. "You're *not* to use matches or fire unless I say that it's safe." "Every time you come to a street, you're to look both ways before crossing." "You're never to swallow a pill a stranger gives you." "If the driver of the car acts drunk, don't get in the car." These are all mandatory limits.

Judy noticed Chris playing by the stove again. He still didn't understand that he was in danger. She took a Wedge of Time, stopped what she was doing, and said, "Chris, you have to play outside of the kitchen while I'm cooking. You and I need to have a talk about why it isn't safe to play close to the stove when food is cooking." She escorted him to the living room with his truck. When she went back to cooking, she thought about how she would get across to Chris the idea that playing by the stove when there are bubbling pots is dangerous.

(b) Flexible Limits

Some limits have no exceptions. However, there are many *flexible limits* that change according to the needs of the situation. "Since we're having company tonight, you may stay up until 9:00. Tomorrow, your bedtime will be the usual 8:00." "Today you're too sick to go to school. This is an exception. Your job is to go to school every day unless you're sick." *Beware that the exception doesn't become the rule!*

As children grow older, limits can be made increasingly flexible. "Now that you're a year older, we can see if you're getting enough sleep by going to bed a half-hour later. Since you're not sleepy, and it's past your regular bedtime, you may read or play quietly with toys in bed." We decide how flexible to be according to what's reasonable in a given situation.

(c) Personal Limits

A third type of limit is a *personal limit* (a choice you offer to your children). "Do you like chocolate, vanilla, or strawberry ice cream?" "What's your favorite color?" "What are your hobbies?" We want to encourage children to develop their personalities by making choices from a wide range of acceptable decisions. "Would you rather wear your blue plaid shirt or your brown shirt?" "Do you want to have carrots, peas, or corn for dinner tonight?"

It isn't acceptable to allow children to go without clothing or eating vegetables, because clothing is necessary and vegetables are an important part of anyone's diet. Which leads me to another key to successful parenting—forcing our personal tastes on our children is unwise; we need to encourage them to make their own choices, within acceptable limits, at an early age. This builds confidence and promotes independence.

The three kinds of limits are (1) Mandatory—"You're never to set fire to trash cans!"; (2) Flexible—"You're to have your homework finished by dinnertime at 6 P.M."; and (3) Personal—"You may decide which of your dress-up clothes you'll wear to the party."

Of Course I Never Told My Son Not to Join a Gang

When Eileen arrived at The Parent Connection, she told a sad story of how her son, Rick, had joined the 96th Street Crips, one of the most violent gangs in Los Angeles. I asked her if she had ever set a limit with him about gangs. She didn't understand. I asked her if she ever said to him, "Rick, you're never to join a gang." She astonished me by saying, "Of course not! He went through the DARE Program. There wasn't any reason to believe that he would join a gang."

DARE, an anti-drug program in schools sponsored by the police department, teaches children about the dangers of drugs and the value of staying away from them. The fact that Eileen needed to supplement the DARE program by setting limits of her own didn't occur to her. Not joining a gang is a mandatory limit. This is an issue that is too serious to be flexible about or to leave to any child's personal choice.

Examples of setting limits using the Three Ws are:

"You're to wash the dishes immediately after dinner."
"You may go outside to play when your room is clean."
"You're never to drive a car when you're intoxicated."
"It's okay for you to have your friends over when your parents are here."
"If someone offers you marijuana or any other illegal drug, you're to say 'No!' every time."
"Your job is to go to school every day. You're to be on time for every class and to keep up with your homework as your teachers require it."

Most parents I've observed find it difficult to be clear about rules and setting limits with their children. They certainly *think* they're being clear, but they're not. I've done research at The Parent Connection with the parents of gang members, dropouts, pregnant teens, drug addicts, and children involved in grand-theft auto and other anti-social behaviors. The majority of these parents don't have a clue about setting limits. When we practice in class, I've discovered they don't know how! Nor do they know how to use the Three Steps I've outlined here. When parents role-play, most lead with a question and immediately start a power contest, insult the child, or jump into a diatribe.

Children are confused when they don't know their limits or boundaries. Wanda, Irene, and Jessie are actual parents from our classes who had no idea how to set limits. Wanda would give Tanika a religious lecture. Eileen lamely said, "Well I guess you're going to do what you're going to do." Jessie was overly-critical, a master put-down artist.

It's reassuring for children to be told firmly, "Yes, this rule is important and must be obeyed." If you get resistance, you may not have explained your reasons behind the rule well enough, or perhaps your child has questions you need to answer. He or she may have overriding personal reasons to behave differently. You need to use your best communication skills to find out where the resistance is so that you can both participate in reaching the best solution to the problem.

Remember, children's nature is to want what they want when they want it. Ultimately, what any responsible person wants is whatever is in a child's best interest. It's up to *you* to decide what's in your children's best interest until they're mature enough to be on their own. You decide what to do according to the needs of the situation. If there's no time to process the resistance now, insist on compliance and tell the child *we* will talk about it later—and *do talk about it later*.

Directive leadership for effective parenting is *proactive*, that is, it is thought through ahead of time with the end results in mind. It's also confident and firm. A structured environment where everyone's rights are respected and protected by specific boundaries provides security and peace of mind for all family members.

Do the incessant power contests at your house exhaust you? Is your family competitive, each person attempting to win at another's expense? Competition belongs on the playing field, not in the family. It's not in anyone's best interest to outwit or outmuscle a family member. Responsibility should be the grand winner, not an ego contest of "I'm better than you!"

The goal of Step II is to help children become clear about what behavior is expected of them, even if they don't understand the reasons completely (Step I). Giving clear directions requires being very specific.

When Gerry came to The Parent Connection, he reported a nasty situation where he had told Sandy (10), "Clean your room." He became furious when she did little to comply, but in class he realized he hadn't provided her with enough information about what "clean your room" meant. He assumed she knew what he meant, but he ignored an important parenting secret—children need repetition. Clear directions give parents predictable results from children, and repetition helps children learn to assume responsibility.

It would be better for Gerry to say, "You're to clean up your room before noon, Sandy. Take your dirty sheets to the laundry and put new ones on the bed, pick up your toys and clothes, dust all your furniture, and vacuum the floor." Gerry can tell if Sandy needs this repetition by observing how thorough she carries out the directions. It is irritating to hear a repetition of something that is already understood. Let the needs of the situation guide you in your use of repetition.

Many parents shortcut the part of their description that tells the child exactly what he or she is to do, so the child has no choice but to interpret what the parent might have intended. The child's version of your request may be very different indeed. No wonder there are so many disagreements.

Another breakthrough for parents is to understand that when children know better, they do better. If you understand this concept, you're exceptional. Even if Sandy had successfully cleaned her room several times before, the issue is not that she hasn't ever done the job. The issue is that she's not doing the job now. There must be a reason why she's not being consistent with her past behavior. People are complex. They think and feel about many different things. Sandy may be depressed or worried, or she may not feel well. In this given situation, if she knew better, she would do better.

And you'll do better in your relationships with your children, when you know how to be a more skillful parent. Probe any problem situation to find out what's really going on with your children. Merely having your children repeat what they're supposed to do may not be the right direction, but you'll never go wrong if you receptively listen to them. Many problems call for a subtle dance between you and your children.

Prepare for Outings by Being Proactive

With proactive planning, you can prevent disasters before they occur. You can avoid a lot of tension away from home if you're proactive and prepare children ahead of time. Tell them where and why they're going, how long you'll be there, who will be there, what there is to do, and how they'll be expected to act. Children need to have specific instructions about how to act. Use this method when visiting the homes of friends or relatives, going to a store or restaurant, or on a special occasion like a wedding or funeral.

Find ways to make it an outing that everyone will enjoy. Here are some proven tips to consider:

- Take along entertaining books or toys if the adult activities will be boring for children.
- Pack a few snacks to avoid complaints about hunger pangs.
- Five or ten minutes before departure, warn children that you're about to leave.
- Avoid embarrassing your children in front of other people.
- Treat your children with respect by preparing them for what you expect them to do; this goes a long way toward making your trip or visit a pleasant one.
- On the way home, you have a captive audience and a perfect time to "catch them being good." Ignore the little things that went wrong and tell them what was right about the outing. Positive acknowledgment reinforces good behavior.

A Proactive Success

Gerry and Maxine planned to take Jason, Jennifer, and Sandy to Aunt Sara and Uncle George's house. The children understood that the visit would be fun and relaxing because they'd be with cousins their own age. There'd be pets to play with and a park nearby.

On the other hand, when they went to Gerry's parents for dinner on Sunday, they would be dressed up. They'd have to be careful not to break anything. They'd be able to play actively outside, but inside they could only play with the quiet toys they'd brought along.

On the drive home Gerry and Maxine explained to each child what he or she did to make the trip more enjoyable. They didn't mention mistakes, unless there was something that was truly inappropriate. If this was the case, they ended on a positive note of encouragement for the child. This activity was Step III in action—Follow Through.

➡ Step III: Follow Through

➡ Step II: Setting Limits

Step I: Teach Right From Wrong

In Step II you give specific explanations of what you expect from your children and when you expect it. Following through is a very important next step. You need to let your children know that you mean what you say and you care enough to see that the rules are carried out. Then let them know if they have or haven't met your expectations. You want your children to develop self-discipline so that they'll internalize right from wrong. Gerry and Maxine used good follow-through.

It's just unbelievable how many parents stumble on Step III or miss it altogether. You must pay attention to whether your children understand you! They need to have reassurance that they're doing it right. You must be prepared to "catch them being good." Catch them in the act of succeeding and tell them about it. "Good for you!" "That's right!" "Terrific, you did it!" Nothing succeeds like success. Children achieve R=TLC only by practical experience. This is another indication that you're moving in the right direction. Hooray! And remember your goal—remember the method of *tender loving care.*

Compliance

When children comply with the limit, they need to have the reassurance that they are doing it right. Acknowledging the right behavior is an important way to demonstrate to children they've understood their parents.

Gerry saw that Sandy made an all-out effort to clean her room by noon. "Sandy, look how all your hard work paid off. Good for you!"

Global Praise Is Too Slick—It Doesn't Stick

Global praise isn't as well understood or appreciated as *specific praise* which uses statement sentences. "You're such a good girl." "You're the best son in the world." With such global praise, children may not feel "I'm good" or "I'm the best," and they'll reject what they think is false. However, they'll readily accept that they did a good job on a task when you acknowledge it *specifically.* The proof is right there. Describe exactly what the child did right. "You wiped up all the spilt milk, and the table is clean again." And later, "Hooray! Tonight there was no spilt milk at the table, and dinner was much more pleasant." Parents have reached breakthrough when they reward their children's successes with specific praise. This skill is one of the most valuable tools parents can use.

Avoid global criticism, too. "You're bad. You never think before you act (ugh!)." Global criticism attacks the person and doesn't address the behavior. Remember this parenting secret—it is vitally important to describe the *behavior* of the child as right or wrong, not the *child* as a good or bad person.

Unfortunately, most parents are much more likely to "catch them being bad." These parents believe that if they point out children's mistakes or embarrass them, that somehow they'll be motivated to improve. Not so. This can diminish children's self-esteem and erode confidence. Another key to successful parenting is understanding that if children see themselves as failures, they'll attract failure; if they see themselves as successes, they'll attract more success. Develop the habit of following through and being quick to acknowledge your children's success.

Partial Compliance

Most parents, when they see a partially-completed job, will immediately start the conversation with what is wrong. This is a bad strategy. Always start with something that is right about your child's efforts.

Sandy partially cleaned her room. Gerry says, "I see that you've picked up your toys and clothes and vacuumed the floor. The room looks much better. You'll be finished when your bed is made, the dresser top is straightened, and the trash is taken out. This isn't much work. It's ten minutes to twelve. You still have time to be finished before noon. Let me know when you're done."

Follow-through is necessary to get the job done of disciplining your children with love and to accomplish the work you've set in motion in Steps I and II. "Sandy, your room looks neat and clean now. I can see that you worked hard and you finished before noon. Good for you!"

No Compliance

If your child fails to accomplish anything, I recommend that you take the time to learn what your child is thinking, not just assume that you know. Go back to Step I and discuss what is going on.

Gerry says, "Sandy, it's noon and I don't see any sign that you've even started on your room."

"You don't make Jennifer and Jason clean their rooms. They get away with everything and I'm the one who has to do all the work."

As Gerry receptively listens, he realizes that Sandy uses the same standards for her two younger siblings. She thinks what's fair is the same as what's equal. "I see. You want to be treated fairly, Sandy. You're saying that it isn't fair for you to clean your room if Jennifer and Jason don't have to clean up their room."

"Yes," Sandy asserts.

"Then what you would like to happen is that the three of you are treated equally."

"That's right."

"That means that you'll go to bed at 7:30 tonight."

"No way," Sandy said incredulously.

"It's equal...and you can also play with Jason's toys," Gerry said with a twinkle in his eye. Sandy started to laugh. Gerry said, "Each of us contributes according to what he or she is able to do. Jennifer and Jason help us keep their room clean, but they're too young to do as much as you. You're ten. They're three and five. Do you still think that it's unfair?"

"No...but I don't want to clean my room now."

"When is the best time for you?"

"Later this afternoon?"

"Sandy, your room needs serious attention. I don't want to go through all this again. We have company coming for dinner tonight. They'll be here at 5:30 P.M. We want the house to be clean by then. We leave by 12:30 to be at your soccer game by 1:00, and there won't be time afterwards. What's your plan?"

"I guess I have to do it now."

"That sounds like a fine plan to me. Let me know when you're finished. By the way, I like it when you tell me what you think is unfair. That way we can figure out what's fair and no one feels mistreated." Dad gave her a hug and sweetened the deal by saying, "Let's get an ice cream cone after the game!" "All right!" Sandy gleefully responded.

Father chose to negotiate with Sandy by explaining the facts. The following sections suggest more techniques to help you resolve conflict and bring back cooperation.

Natural Consequences

Some lessons are better taught by experience, which is still one of the best teachers. This type of learning rapidly builds youngsters' thinking skills. Except when a child is in an unsafe situation, it might be best to let nature take its course.

Natural consequences involve the predictability of nature. For example, if you go into the cold without gloves, your hands will become cold. Being late to a movie means you don't see the beginning. Leaving a bike in the rain results in rust. Eating too much can give you a stomach ache. If you step on glass with bare feet, you'll get cut. If you touch fire, you'll get burned.

Children need many opportunities to interact with nature in order to understand the world. When Chris fell off his bicycle, he learned something about balance and gravity. These lessons are vital to building rational development and good thinking skills. Children who watch six hours of television per day don't have time to socialize in extended play. They also don't have time for activities to make their bodies strong or for reading, hobbies, or simply thinking (3-T Rule). I recommend that parents keep control of the TV, and while we're at it, also control the "sugar bowl." Sugar and too many refined foods are other sources of child development problems. Excess sugar naturally causes behavior problems in children and makes it difficult for them to concentrate.

Logical Consequences

With *logical consequences*, there's a direct cause-and-effect relationship between two events. For example, if Larry teases until his friend is angry, he'll cause his friend to want to leave. If a toy is broken on purpose, then it's logical that the toy won't be replaced with a new one right away. Carelessly spilling a drink means you don't get a refill. Not putting the bike away means you can't ride it for a day. Refusing to brush your teeth means no candy or soft drinks. If brother and sister argue and fuss, they'll have to play separately. Refusing to eat a well-balanced dinner means going without dessert. Not doing homework means you can't watch TV. "Grandma's Rule" is a time-honored technique to understand logical consequences.

Grandma's Rule

Grandma's Rule is "We work before we play." This is a clever, logical way to teach children responsibility. All children seek immediate gratification. "I want what I want when I want it." Learning to delay gratification is an important part of growing up. And Grandma's Rule works!

Remember how frustrated Kirk's parents were when he didn't clean up after his snack? You might be thinking, but what can I do about a situation like that? Grandma's Rule is perfect. Calling it "Grandma's Rule" implies wisdom and experience; it's a sound way to get jobs done and establish routines around the house. Grandma's Rule says it's logical to work before having fun. Because it's the nature of children to want to have fun all the time, this rule isn't automatic for them. When work (the painful part) comes before play (the pleasure part), children can look forward to a built-in reward for their efforts. The key is to make work enjoyable and help them see the wisdom of work first, reward later.

Patience is also important for parents. In spite of the almost paranoid belief among parents that children are out to "get us," in reality they're mostly motivated to meet their immediate needs. Cleaning up after themselves hardly qualifies as one of their "needs." Kirk's parents could, using patience, remind him that cleaning up goes with eating a snack. There's no TV until he does so.

Other ways to apply Grandma's Rule are:

- "Clean your room before you play outside."
- "When your homework is finished, you can watch TV."
- "Eat your vegetables, and then you may have dessert."
- "Do your homework before playing with your toys."

Over time, Grandma's Rule can do wonders for maintaining order around the house. Try it for a week and see the results!

G r a n d m a ' s   R u l e :
We Work Before We Play

The Wedge of Time

As introduced earlier, the Wedge of Time is a period of time to relax and figure out a solution to conflict. The amount of time depends on the needs of the situation. One sure way to tell if more time is needed is if you or any other interested party is angry. Angry people are afraid and aren't as likely to respond with their best thinking or in loving ways. They tend to blame the closest person, most likely *you*. Then power struggles escalate. Time is a great healer, however. By taking time out, you can get control of your emotions and plan what to say and do.

This technique doesn't mean that once everyone is in a good mood you should just forget the problem. With everyone calm and relaxed, you can now get to work on the problem. The Thinking Chair is one example of how to use a Wedge of Time.

The Thinking Chair: "Time Out"

Tommy (6) wrestles his tricycle away from Freddie. He kicks Freddie and uses foul language. Paul, Tommy's father, brings Tommy inside and promptly tells him to sit in his Thinking Chair. He sets the kitchen timer for six minutes, placing it where Tommy can see it.

Paul says, "Tommy, sit here until the timer goes off. You're to figure out your problem and how you're going to solve it." (Note: If Dad has not employed Step I—Teaching Right from Wrong and Step II—Setting Limits, then Tommy should not be disciplined in this way.)

Paul leaves Tommy alone to think. This "Wedge of Time" allows both Paul and Tommy time to reflect, and it's also a good stress-reducer. When the timer goes off, Paul calmly asks Tommy, "Okay, what's the problem?"

"Freddie took my tricycle and wouldn't let me ride it, so I smacked him," answers Tommy, pouting self-righteously. Dad receives Tommy's logic. "I see. You think that when Fred didn't give you your tricycle back, you didn't have any choice but to fight with him. I thought I heard some bad language, too!"

"I called him a dirty _____ , because he is," Tommy snarls.

"So if people don't do what you say, then it's okay to kick and use bad language?"

Tommy replies, "No."

"Then there must be a better way for you to handle a problem like that," states Dad.

"I don't know."

"Do you need more time to think about it?"

"No."

At this point, Paul recognizes that Tommy doesn't know an appropriate way to solve this problem, so he helps him out. "The problem is that Freddie took your tricycle and wouldn't give it back?"

"Yes," Tommy sulks.

"Did you tell Freddie that you wanted your tricycle back?"

"No."

"Why not?"

"Because he's just selfish. It's *my* tricycle."

"Tommy, we need to have you practice saying what you want, so your friends can understand. The best way is to use strong words that are respectful. If you said, 'Freddie, I want to ride my tricycle now. This is my tricycle and your time is up,' do you think he'd give it back to you?"

"Maybe."

"Try it. If it doesn't work, let me know and we'll figure out something else to do. You're not to kick and use bad language to get what you want. You need to find a better way to solve your problems. Okay?"

"Okay."

"How about a hug? I like the way we can solve problems."

The Thinking Chair is for children between the ages of 3 and 12 who have misbehaved. Tell them to sit in a chair in an isolated area—without toys, television, playmates, or other distractions—for a specific span of time. A good rule of thumb is one minute of Time Out for every year of age.

If you are introducing the Thinking Chair to your child for the first time, it's best to explain what it is and the rules for its use. When the child is naughty, tell him or her to sit in the chair you've designated. Be sure to place the chair within range of supervision, but away from distractions. Most of us can visualize "Dennis the Menace" sitting in his rocking chair in the corner, where he was sent to think about his misdeeds. We don't have to use a corner for the chair; because your motive is not to shame your child. It's to create an opportunity for him or her to think through a problem. So, the middle of the room or the grass in a park is fine, too.

The best environment to promote "thinking" is a quiet one. It's a good idea to set a timer as the impersonal time keeper. Place it out of reach of the child but where he or she can see and hear it. Don't just say, "Sit there until I tell you to get up." A telephone call or an interesting project may cause you to forget your child. Try to avoid being punitive or inviting power contests, because this method becomes useless if it builds hostility and resentment.

The Thinking Chair method of discipline has the advantage of allowing parents to engage in problem solving with their children by encouraging thinking skills. Parents expect the child to:

- Identify the problem, and
- Figure out a solution.

It's exciting to see children learning to be creative in their reasoning. Your goal is to teach your children to be more responsible by helping them sort out which solutions are appropriate and which are not. You're creating an opportunity for them to expand their thinking.

Far superior to spanking, the Thinking Chair reduces a child's hostility toward his or her parent. Children who have just been spanked have their attention on the "mean parent," not on what they did to cause the spanking. Time Out in the Thinking Chair avoids an unnecessary diversion of "I'm mad at you," and enables children to focus on the cause of the problem. Children soon return to doing something more enjoyable.

Moving the child from an activity to isolation makes boredom a source of discomfort. Children prefer being occupied with friends, watching TV, or other pursuits more than sitting still with nothing to do but pass time.

For a six-year-old, six minutes in the Thinking Chair is usually long enough. When the timer rings, the child understands that he or she is going to be asked for certain information:

"What's the problem?"
"And what's the solution?"

You want to make sure your child understands what behavior was wrong or inappropriate. If he or she hasn't figured it out, keep the explanation short and age-appropriate. Then ask for a solution. At that point, a promise is required that the offending behavior will be changed or not repeated. The promise is a verbal contract that "I" will use a better way to solve this kind of problem in the future.

After you've finished the discussion with your child, follow through by showing your love and affection with words and a hug. Express your pleasure at how the child has solved the problem. After the child has experienced some discomfort and has thought things over, parents need to follow through with acknowledgment—catch the child being good! This is the most important technique parents have in helping their children become leaders and not mere followers.

The Thinking Chair is extremely effective because it usually stops the inappropriate behavior immediately. However, what about those times it doesn't? If the problem persists, double the amount of time in the Thinking Chair, and repeat the two questions. If this still doesn't work, another form of Time Out is to have your child play in his or her room, a distraction with a different kind of Wedge of Time. A change of attitude will usually occur with good stress-management techniques.

There are many variations on the Thinking Chair method. How the variations are used depends upon a child's age and the circumstances. Other versions of Time Out are "go to your room," "take a nap," or "grounding" an older child to the house. Parents have used these Time Out techniques for centuries, and they're as successful today as ever.

By the way, do *you* have a Thinking Chair, a place where you go to figure out the problem and the solution? If you don't, you need to designate a place where you have peace and quiet just to think. The 3-T Rule—Thinking Takes Time—is not only for children but for parents, too. It leads us to a big parenting secret—the more you're proactive (thinking ahead) rather than reactive (thinking on the spot), the more successful you'll be with your children and other aspects of your life. Another benefit is that you'll have less stress.

The Look

You know the "look" I mean. It's a look from a parent to a child that says "I'm paying attention to you." "I disapprove." "This is serious." Some people call it "The Eye"—a glare that includes body language which says, "I mean business!" The parent may move toward the child, shaking their head slowly or flashing a thumbs-down sign to emphasize "No."

A firmly-expressed repetition of a parent's rule may accompany The

Look if the child doesn't comply. Responsible parents use a lot of different warnings with children. The "look," accompanied by "Think about what you're doing," can turn around a potentially undesirable situation in a hurry.

Move In

This is a disciplinary technique that most school teachers have down pat. Move in. Stand very close. Or stand directly behind your child. Moving in gets a child's attention *fast*. All of us have about a three-foot radius of body space that projects away from us. Most of us feel safe when people stay out of our body space (keep their distance). We become very aware when someone closes in on us. It makes our hair stand on end to have someone position themselves directly behind us. Many a child has been propelled to compliance by this very simple technique of moving in.

Another technique that helps with discipline is to avoid asking your child to come to you. Instead, *go to the child*. The dynamic is entirely different. Your body language communicates more than you might realize. In situations that are not disciplinary in nature, ask the child to come to you.

Moving in can also add an intimate, rewarding, bonding dimension to your relationship with children, but it sometimes takes your time to make it effective. Sherryl (10) was uninterested in trading her TV time for other activities. The plan could have fallen apart, but Wanda came up with the idea of playing card and board games with her. While they played games, they talked about other activities Sherryl would like. A new performing dance group was starting nearby. Wanda was relieved when Sherryl joined. Here's an example of how a parent's love can be spelled as T–I–M–E. Wanda's one-on-one attention for a brief time resulted in Sherryl's taking up a rewarding activity.

Ignore

Cassandra, a grandmother, told me that her daughter and husband were frustrated with her grandson, Charlie (5), and his temper tantrums. She described a power-drunk child. I asked her, "What's the purpose of a temper tantrum?" She said, "To get attention." I told her, "The solution to this problem is simple: remove your attention. Ignore him." Use a hands-off leadership style. She was astonished. It had never occurred to any of them to stop fueling the fire.

Babies have temper tantrums because they don't have words to express what they need. As soon as language develops, children can easily be trained to stop the tantrums and to *ask* for what they want. Show the child that there's an easier way to get his or her needs met. Change how you react. When a child asks or behaves appropriately, pay attention. Temper tantrums get *no* attention. Cassandra was on the phone in a flash and told her daughter about this "miracle"—ignore the inappropriate behavior and reward the appropriate behavior; it's another example of "catch them being good." And it works!

Ignoring for short periods of time can be a powerful motivator which brings a child into line. Ignoring means briefly removing all of your attention from the misbehaving child. Don't look at or speak directly to the child. If necessary, walk out of the room, or go into the bathroom and close the door. Don't show anger with your voice or body language. Simply withdraw and be absorbed in another activity such as a magazine or newspaper. Remember, though, pay attention to the child when the offending behavior stops, and don't mention the offensive behavior. It will soon become behavior of the past.

Other behaviors effectively handled with this technique are whining, fussing, loud crying, constant begging or demanding, not taking "No" for an answer, and willful disobedience. Patience and emotional control on your part are necessary to achieve the positive results you want. "Yes, but where do I find that?" If this is still your question, go back to the chapter on stress management.

You May Forget and I May Forget, but a Paper Never Forgets

Contracts are agreements among parents and children that are written by the child, signed by all parties concerned, and posted in an obvious place as a reminder. I've used many contracts with my own children. They clarify thinking and are excellent "reminders" of our agreements.

The *Good Habit Chart* is an excellent way to help children overcome inappropriate habitual behaviors that are hard to change. Do not use this method continually, but use it when other techniques aren't doing the job. Design a simple grid on a piece of paper with the days of the week on top, and the *good* habits you want your child to achieve listed on the left side (put down one difficult habit, one a little less difficult, and three fairly easy behaviors). Draw lines up and down the grid to make daily boxes for each habit.

Keep this secret to yourself—the Good Habit Chart is a *rigged* game. Your child absolutely cannot fail at it because you will see to it that he or she is successful. Whatever you do, don't expect perfection. Even if you have to, add the opportunity to earn "bonus points." An easy point system for the chart is: 2 points (good job), 1 point (fair job), and 0 (not good enough). A very young child can have a smiling face for a good job, a face with a straight line for a mouth for a fair job, and a frowning face for an unsatisfactory job. For a seven-day week of five habits, at a maximum of 2 points each, that makes 70 possible points. Set a goal of 50 points to have your child win a prize, given at the end of the week when the chart points are totaled. The prize could be an activity, a toy, or something special your child would like to do or have. It need not be expensive or elaborate.

Have fun adding up the points each day. Catch your child being good on his or her successes. Encourage your child when efforts weren't quite good enough. The payoff for children is the special daily attention, praise, and encouragement they receive from you, plus the weekly prize. The Good Habit Chart, by the way, also works for adults. It's a great way to "gain" your optimal weight, develop regular exercise habits, or overcome procrastination. This technique works for everyone!

The Family Meeting

This technique—more than any other—made the biggest difference in moving our family away from punishment and into discipline with love. It wasn't easy to start. When I suggested the idea, everyone was totally resistant. I will never forget the first meeting. We all sat down at the dinner table. I had established an agenda. The first item was a particularly painful problem. Everyone started to argue. Robert said, "I don't have to sit here and listen to this." TJ said, "I don't either." Everyone abruptly got up and left the table leaving me by myself. I sighed and walked upstairs to write in my journal. The first thing that I wrote was, "A stumble is a step forward." The next week we had a civilized meeting, the first of many. We began to solve our problems.

Once a week we sat down at the dining room table with the family calendar, old business, new agenda items, pads of paper, and pens to have a Family Meeting. We rotated positions. First, someone read what was on the calendar and added to it new events like school activities, doctor appointments, birthdays, and trips. The second person read the minutes from the last meeting. The third person, who was "chair," went through all of the agenda items, while the fourth person took minutes. We always closed with appreciations and gratitudes.

The Family Meeting helped us plan and organize our lives, as well as anticipate and solve problems. I learned not to start off with an issue that had a lot of heat around it. That was my mistake at our first stumbling effort. If an item was too hot, we might "table" it for the next meeting (Wedge of Time). Sometimes we would have two-way or three-way meetings where people who were in conflict would solve their problems together. These meetings were positive and provided the opportunity to air complaints and express our feelings in a routine and wholesome way. I strongly recommend making use of the Family Meeting on a regular basis. Use it as an opportunity to be democratic when it's reasonable and avoid abusing the opportunity by being authoritarian. The Family Meeting is a chance for all family members to be *heard* .

Family Activities

One of the most important family activities is a sit-down dinner. Dinner needs to be a planned time so other activities can be scheduled around it. I was surprised to hear how few families take the time to eat a meal with everyone present, without a TV going, or without the telephone ringing and other interruptions. Table talk is valuable. One rule for dinner is no unpleasant talk allowed—it's bad for digestion. In our family, we told our MSEs, or "Most Significant Events" of the day, at each dinner. It was a great way to hear what was important for each person.

Successful families plan special events, traditions, and outings with each other. It's a good idea for a parent who has more than one child to spend individual time with each one. It makes each child feel special and provides an opportunity to bond without the competition of siblings.

There isn't any activity that you can do with your children more important than saying, "I love you!" It needs to be said every day, sometimes several times a day. A dad at The Parent Connection told me that his father never told him that he loved him, even though they both knew that the love was there. He said that his father thinks that it isn't masculine to say "I love you" to a son. Today's fathers are breaking away from this notion. Affirming love by actually saying the words is vital for building self-esteem.

Children who feel connected to their parents are inclined to be disciplined. You will be a breakthrough parent when you can keep the feeling and tone of your family positive. Of course, you will need some help from your children to do this!

Leaving Messages

An excellent way to promote discipline and enhance harmony around the house is to set up methods of communicating with each other. By your telephone have several pencils, pens, and pads of paper for messages. Decide on a special place where these messages will be placed. In our family, it was under magnets on the refrigerator. Install a white board with erasable pens. Write your information to family members on the board, and erase the messages when they've been read. This is a great place for reminders and to notify someone of a change of plans. You'll never regret these practical ways of enhancing daily communication among family members.

Willful Disobedience—Do I Get to Hit Her Now?

What if the situation with Sandy, Gerry and Maxine's daughter, didn't turn out that well? What if Gerry got back pure rebellion?

"No, I'm not cleaning up my room. I don't care if I go to soccer and I'm not going to go to school any more. I'm going to hang out with the wrong crowd, drop out of school, and make you a grandparent before your time."

This scenario was used for role-playing in a class which Jessie had attended. "Do I get to hit her now?" Jessie inquired incredulously. In his home, battering was a way of life. You've reached the point where you've done all you know how to do; but how do you handle willful disobedience?

First remember that the goal is R=TLC. Anything you do now can make a big difference. Your goal is cooperation, not more resistance.

Poor Jessie, when he came into the class the only tool he had for raising children was a hammer. Discipline had been very easy for Jessie and his family: if you don't like what your children are doing, hit them! (We'll talk more about hitting in Chapter 11.) In willful disobedience from a simple, "No, I don't want to," to the heavy rebellion of an antisocial teenager, you have many effective techniques to choose from.

Punishment has a long history in child rearing. Whether physical or psychological, punishment has been taken for granted as a necessary teaching tool for generations. In the next chapter we'll explore the wisdom, dynamics, and methods of punishment. We'll look at situations where there's willful disobedience. What choices do you have in reacting to a crisis? And when your child is out of control, how can you best use your leadership skills to take charge of the situation? We'll answer these and other questions about punishment.

❤

CHAPTER ELEVEN

DISCIPLINE
VS.
PUNISHMENT

After Robert and TJ moved into our house, we had a confrontation every day. We didn't have the stomach to measure up to the degree of violence they were used to. One nightmarish evening, I found myself at the limits of my endurance with TJ. He was on a jealous rampage over the fact that I was reading to Robert. Much to my amazement, I threw TJ over his bed and spanked his bottom! He yelled and I yelled. Things seemed better because he was now sulking (at least he was quiet).

I thought about this incident a lot. I was used to maintaining control of thirty or more school children his age in a classroom without ever spanking them. Why weren't the skills I knew how to use in the classroom working for me at home? The difference was that I was facing problems at home that I had never faced at school. The boys thought "might makes right." TJ had such a low self-image that he felt love only when he was treated negatively. In other words, he thought, the way I know I'm loved is when I get punished; therefore, I'll help you love me by being mean, by not sharing, or by not cooperating with reasonable rules of behavior.

My conclusion about what to do to correct this miserable state of affairs was not to use corporal punishment or intimidation. I decided that was the reason why TJ had so little control over his behavior. What TJ and Robert both needed was more discipline. By lovingly teaching right from wrong, setting limits and following through, we were able to avoid the dangers of punishment and heal many of the wounds from the past. By the way, I had no idea how much repetition would be required before our sons would really understand and "know" better, particularly since my husband and I didn't have the advantage of teaching these important lessons to them when they were little and more impressionable.

Raising the Red Flag on Punishment

In this chapter, we will look more in depth at the difference between *discipline* and *punishment*. Many people use these words interchangeably. For the sake of clarity, I mean two different things when I use these words. We've already seen that discipline means to teach responsible behavior. This is done by helping children learn appropriate routines, rules, and regulations to guide their behavior. "Discipline with love" means to teach children with tender loving care how to think clearly, be loving, and confident.

Punishment, on the other hand, means to cause someone to experience pain. It means to make someone suffer. When someone causes us pain or suffering, we feel hurt, angry, revengeful, rejected, or afraid. Punishment attempts to teach children not from a place of love, but from a place of instilling fear. A child's reaction to pain is no different from an adult's. We all instinctively avoid pain whenever we can.

Most parents wrestle with this discipline vs. punishment issue on a daily basis. It helps to think the matter through ahead of time so that you'll have a plan of action when the inevitable happens and your child disobeys. When this kind of behavior occurs, do you want to choose discipline or punishment?

Why Make Children Feel Pain?

Either physical or psychological punishment can lessen the likelihood that undesirable behavior will be repeated. Punishment can have strong and lasting effects in stopping undesirable behavior. Anyone who has touched fire will not touch fire again. Because pain can be such an effective teacher, does it mean that we should rely on it as so many parents do?

Punishment indicates only what *not* to do, not what *to* do. This is important. Too many parents "catch them being bad," and leave it at that. Children, or you for that matter, won't automatically know what to do about a situation when we're told that what we're doing is not correct.

Donna repeatedly tells her son, "Put that down. Stop that. Stop making so much noise." Her commands don't give her son enough information about what the problem is, which is that her four-year-old was practicing to be a drummer. What if she said, "Your drumming bothers me. I don't feel up to listening right now. You can either put the drum up while you're in the house, or you can play with it in the backyard." In this case, Donna could avoid the confusion and restore her peace of mind.

Lessons taught by using punishment can backfire, causing results far different from those intended. The bonding between a parent and a child is undermined by punishment because the parent is viewed as a person the child cannot trust. All people will try to avoid or to escape from anyone who punishes them. The punisher becomes associated with pain.

Joel told me, "If I tell my old man the truth, I'll get clobbered. So why tell him the truth? If he finds out that I lied, I'll still get it, but lots of times he doesn't find out. What he doesn't know won't hurt *me!*"

Punishment models aggression, not assertiveness. It encourages talking with fists rather than talking with words. With too much punishment, children will talk with their feet and leave! Children imitate aggressive acts in their relationships with each other and, when grown, with adults and, eventually, even with their own children.

Psychological Punishment

Psychological punishment is the most overlooked way that people are caused pain and suffering. There are no visible bruises, welts or scars, yet the trauma of the experience can have devastating long-term effects. It can cause people to lose confidence and lower self-esteem. Being told that you're bad, a pest, unworthy, and unlovable cuts deep into the psyche. These bad thoughts are stored in the subconscious mind and will come back to cause distorted thinking, unloving feelings for oneself and others, and either a lack of confidence or false confidence. In other words, psychological punishment undermines a person's ability to respond appropriately.

Brad never stands up straight. He hangs his head and has long red hair that covers his freckled face. When we were doing the self-esteem lesson, he told us that his dad's nickname for him was "Ugly." "Come here, Ugly. Ugly, it's time for you to go to bed." His father never liked Brad's red hair and numerous freckles. Consequently, neither did Brad. They were features over which Brad had no control, and he continued to perceive them as a permanent disfigurement.

Steve said, "My father could make me feel lower than a snake's belly: 'If you think he's so cute, take him.' 'If he had a brain, he'd be dangerous.' 'He's only good when he's asleep.'" Every relationship Steve has had as an adult has ended up as a miserable failure. Now he has two daughters and the children's mother doesn't want him to see them.

Before my husband and I adopted him, our son Robert experienced heavy psychological intimidation. He was often told, "If you don't knock it off, I'll punch your lights out. If you don't like the rules, there's the door—you won't be missed."

When parents talk to their children like this, it makes a deep and long-lasting impression. Words can hurt! Psychological punishment induces hate for the person who administers the punishment, but most of all it creates self-loathing. "If I'd been a better person, my parents would have loved me more."

With such unhappy side effects, it's amazing that parents continue to cause their children to suffer. Many actually think that they're doing their children a favor. They don't realize that there's a better way: disciplining with love. The way to show love is to not play on a child's normal fears.

Corporal Punishment

Corporal or *physical punishment* is any method used to cause physical pain such as hitting, pulling hair, pinching, and biting. Of course, it's rare that physical punishment is used at the exclusion of psychological punishment. Most children get hit by both. The most common method of corporal punishment is spanking.

Spanking is a subject of controversy for a number of reasons. To begin with, there are no guidelines. Nobody agrees on just what a spanking is or on what's acceptable—how much, how hard, how often, and with what means (a hand, paddle, etc.). People disagree, too, as to when spanking becomes beating or abuse. Spanking, however, relies on children's fear as a motivator, and fear is an emotion we need to resolve, not escalate.

Child abuse and neglect has reach unprecedented levels in the United States and around the world. After working with over 7,000 parents who were in legal trouble, I've found that some form of abuse and neglect was frequently a contributing factor. I believe that the "rise" in abuse and neglect is due to an increased awareness on the part of policy makers that punishment causes damage to children. There's considerable research on this subject, the results of which most parents are not privileged to know.

Most parents say that the methods they use to chastise their children are mild in comparison to what *they* experienced from their own parents. Since most parents rarely receive any formal training to be good parents, it's easy to "break the law." For example, if you had no training on how to drive a car, or what the laws are for safe driving, you'd be likely to have an accident or get a ticket for unsafe driving. You'd be told that ignorance of the law is no excuse.

There are countless laws about how children are to be treated. I don't know of any parent in my class that had instruction on these laws until they were in trouble. Burt was one of our fathers that said, "I didn't know that it was against the law to spank your child." Actually, it's not against the law to spank a child, but it's against the law to leave bruises and welts, which is what Burt had done. He used a belt. I've found that, like Burt, most parents tend to minimize what they did to punish their children. Part of the problem is knowing what is a *spanking* and what is a *beating!* Where one stops and another starts is not clear.

On the one hand, we have an unwritten law in our society that no one has a right to tell us how to raise our children. But on the other hand, there are numerous *written* laws that specifically state how children are to be treated. Most parents are astounded at how fast the authorities can, and do, remove children from their homes because of what they took to be a routine spanking.

Teachers, physicians, and childcare workers have a legal responsibility to report any suspicion of child endangering. If a child comes to school with welt marks or unexplained bruises, professionals must report this or pay a large fine, face time in jail, or even lose their licenses or credentials. It's in everyone's best interest that children are safe and are treated responsibly.

One reason that authorities are called to intervene is that "spanking" can easily get out of control. In the dialogue below we can see how this can happen (the following is taken directly from one of our Parent Connection classes):

Mark: Charlene (17) broke into her mom's house and stole jewelry and CDs. She was expelled from high school and is in continuation school. She isn't doing very well there.

Jayne: How did you end up in a crisis?

Mark: I hadn't really spanked her in a year or so. I raised them on that kind of thing. She developed a smart mouth. I was confronting her about her not having done her chores. I warned her two times, "I won't accept foul language from you. If you want to keep that up, I'll get physical." She looked at me straight in the eye and started in with the obscenities. I walked out and got the belt that I've used for a lot of years. I told her to stick her nose in the corner and she's going to get it. I counted ten quick ones on the fanny. That's not devastating. That's a good amount. That's a spanking. She pretty much resented it.

Jayne: I would resent it, too, if I were 17 and my father forced me to stick my nose in a corner and get spanked with a belt. In fact, I would resent it no matter how old I was. When you say that Charlene pretty much resented the treatment, what did she do to show it? Did she go after revenge?

Mark: I guess she did. She told her counselor the next day and the police were called. We were ordered into family counseling and I was told to come to these classes. I hope you don't think that spanking's wrong. I think spanking is an end all in itself. Isn't there a place in our society for spanking as part of a wholesome, all-around method for raising children?

Jayne: There are very few professional parent educators who encourage spanking. We know that there are so many better ways to get your point across.

Mark: Hitting is an expression of love. If you withhold spankings, then you hate your child. Parents spank because they love their child. What about "spare the rod and spoil the child?" If you don't hit, then you aren't showing love.

Jayne: I hope you'll give this idea some more thought. I see serious problems with thinking of spanking as an expression of love. The problem with "spare the rod and spoil the child" is that people don't know what a "rod" is—a belt, a wooden spoon, an extension cord, a switch, or a hand? How much spanking is okay? It's open for interpretation how much to swat—one, five, ten swats, or more? "Spare the rod and spoil the child" is a Biblical metaphor that suggests that if we don't discipline our children when they're young, they'll grow up to be "spoiled" or irresponsible citizens. I couldn't agree more with that interpretation. I know that children can grow up to make us proud of them without us resorting to hitting them.

Mark: When I would spank my kids, it was for something that they did that was definitely wrong. It can be used as a tool to divert them away from danger or in a case of willful disobedience. Immediately after the spanking, I'd make my children tell me what they were getting spanked for. Afterward, love was confirmed. Physical love, hugging, and calming down.

Jayne: Mark, we know that there are women who expect their husbands to beat them. They say that it shows them that they're loved. Do you think that Charlene is a candidate to be one of these women? Mark, suppose that the law said that no parent under *any* circumstances was ever allowed to strike children in any way. How would you raise your daughters so they'd grow up to be responsible? Will you spend some time this week thinking about this?

By the end of the course, Mark had rethought his position on spanking. He also had more tools to use which helped him break his reliance on spanking. He reported that his relationship with his daughters had improved dramatically. He had substituted his reliance on physical pain for assertive communication, receptive listening, and "I" statements. His daughters were being treated with dignity and respect. What a difference it made!

Spanking is one of the least desirable ways to discipline children. Picture Sammy, who has just been spanked for hitting his little brother. He's crying and he's angry. Who is Sammy angry at? At the parent who spanked him. His mind is completely removed from the reason he was spanked. Furthermore, he's in such a bad mood he won't listen to a lecture on why he "deserved" to be hit. He hit, he was hit for hitting; naturally, he's confused.

In a research study I worked on, where 400 parents of four-year-old children were interviewed, we asked, "Do you hit your child?" We were surprised by the range of answers we got.

Dave answered, "Yes." When I asked how often, he said, "I think she got a spanking last year."

Sharon responded with, "She gets an average of four spankings a day." Sharon is an example of what is meant by "If the only tool you have is a hammer, then every problem looks like a nail." Sharon didn't have much in her toolbox. She didn't understand Step I—teaching right from wrong—or setting limits, catch them being good, Grandma's Rule, or the Wedge of Time.

I met Sharon's daughter when she got off the school bus. She was adorable, and naturally she deserved better. She just doesn't know more mature ways to behave yet. Sharon is another mother who believes in the "Board of Education," that spanking is teaching.

Hitting teaches aggression and violence. The message that "hitting is wrong" gets lost. I think children lose much of their ability to understand right from wrong when they're hit. Hitting becomes an end in itself, precisely what Mark said in class.

Some children would rather "get it over with" than be lectured to. Without an explanation (Step I), children often don't understand why they were spanked. Children need to learn early how to discern what is or is not correct behavior. Adults don't reason well when they're angry, and neither do children.

One of my favorite cartoons is *Calvin and Hobbes.* In one strip, Calvin's mother gets dressed up to go shopping. As she leaves the house, Calvin gleefully squirts her with the garden hose. The last picture shows him walking away, holding his behind. His comment is, "What a grouch she is!" When children are spanked, they rarely think about what *they* did wrong. They focus on what *you* did wrong.

One of the dads in my classes pointed out to me that spanking children is an unfair fight. He said that you wouldn't put a heavyweight in the ring with a lightweight and call it a fair fight. In the case of children, not only is there this big difference in size, but they're not even allowed to defend themselves. They can't fight back! Of course, children can be very clever in getting revenge in other ways, but the truth is that they're not allowed to raise a hand to their parent because the parent thinks that they deserve to be hit because they were bad. If you've ever said, "This hurts me more than it hurts you," you were disciplining wrong.

The breakthrough happens when you know how to discipline effectively from a place of love; if you're coming from love, it doesn't hurt your child. There's no guilt because what you're doing is in the best interests of your child. Your children may not like being disciplined, and they may even feel uncomfortable—no one likes being told that we can't do what we want to do. However, the ultimate feeling is that both the parent and the child are satisfied.

If you're convinced that spanking is necessary in order to raise "unspoiled" children, stop and think about it. Can you get the job done, teaching right from wrong, without it? By adding more tools, you probably can. The Three Steps of disciplining with love can do wonders. Some people think, "But you don't know *my* children," or that I'm advocating a "permissive approach." Children respond to the way they're treated. If their treatment is built on fear, they'll reflect it. The point I'm making is that the tender loving care method gets better results. This doesn't mean permissiveness. Countless parents have raised their children to responsible adulthood and never used either psychological or corporal punishment. It *is* possible!

The Aggressive Child

Morris comes from a family where violence is the rule. His youngest boy Brian (7) was uncontrollable. Brian was suspended from school for hitting, spitting, and tearing the blouse of a teacher who was trying to stop his attack on another boy in class. Morris was astonished when I said that Brian is afraid. "How can he be afraid? He fears no one!" I repeated that aggressive children are afraid. They feel unsafe. They fear for their survival. They're afraid of being abandoned. These fears come from not having their basic needs met. There's a wide range of aggressive behaviors: hitting, biting, hostile teasing, choking, provoking, pulling hair, sassy back talk to adults, mistreating pets, angry screaming, slapping, not sharing, pinching, throwing toys (or dirt, rocks, sticks), scolding, destroying things, excessive risk-taking, kicking, threatening to harm others, spitting, and swearing.

Aggressive children don't see how they fit in the world in constructive ways. Many children who become aggressive are afraid to express their true feelings. Parents must learn to become receptive listeners. Being able to talk about feelings goes a long way toward solving problems, as Morris and Mark found out with their children.

One of the best ways to handle aggressive children is to separate them from the object of their anger and give them a Wedge of Time. A Thinking Chair or some other Time Out method can be used. Once the child has calmed down, find a quiet time to sit down and listen to what is bothering the child. By addressing only the symptoms (i.e., the aggressive behavior) and ignoring the fear that the child experiences, we fail to solve the problem. The child's concerns must be addressed directly if they're to be solved. If the problem persists, you will not regret getting some professional help.

Obviously, a parent who has an aggressive child needs to ask if he or she is modeling the very behavior that they're objecting to. Children learn ways of handling frustration and rage from their parents. Many people think being aggressive is acceptable for an adult and is unacceptable for a child. The truth is, aggressiveness is inappropriate for anyone at any age. Children will do what you do, and will mistrust you if what you say is different.

The best guide for disciplining a child is to follow the Golden Rule: "Do unto others as you would have them do unto you." If you were out of control and irresponsible, wouldn't you want to be reassured that you're safe and shown how to get your needs met? Wouldn't you want someone to care enough to understand your pain and help you avoid it?

Danny (4) is jealous of his baby sister. He made hostile advances toward her on two occasions. His mother and father told him that he was never to hurt his sister. As his mother, Gretchen, walked into the baby's bedroom, she was horrified to see Danny biting the baby's arm so hard that it bled.

She pulled Danny away from the crib, then she comforted and took care of the baby. Next, she took Danny firmly by the hand, escorted him out of the room, and sat him in a chair. She said, "You're *never* to bite your sister. I'm going to bite you so you can see how much it hurts." Gretchen bit Danny firmly, not puncturing the skin but hard enough that Danny didn't like it. She restricted Danny from being with the baby for the rest of the day.

Sometimes parents need to demonstrate to children that their behavior hurts others. Young children don't have empathy and sympathy. These emotions require being able to generalize that the feelings or emotions *you* have are just like the feelings I have. They don't connect the act of biting with pain. It's up to us to say, "How would you like to be bitten?"—and teach them that biting can hurt.

Do you think that when Gretchen showed Danny that biting hurts, not by actually causing pain but by putting enough pressure that he associates teeth with pain, that she was punishing him? I don't think so. It's unlikely that she has caused him to experience undue pain or suffering. I say that it's discipline.

Gretchen went on to listen receptively to Danny as he communicated how he feels displaced by his sister. She used sympathy and empathy to understand his point of view. She followed up by teaching him why it's wrong to bite his sister (Golden Rule). Then she showed him ways that he could play with his sister where they could have fun together and ways that he could take part in caring for her appropriately.

Children must not be allowed to defy parents when they're clearly in the wrong. This is the time to take charge with direct leadership.

Other Behavior Problems

Aggression is not the only way children express rage. Children may, instead, exhibit the following list of behaviors: pouting, sulking, being irritable, bad moods, failing to do chores or to participate in household tasks, excessive people-pleasing, being fearful, being timid or passive, and withdrawing (e.g., exclusively watching TV, reading, or being isolated in a bedroom).

Children who demonstrate these behaviors do not need Time Out. They need to have attention paid *immediately* to the problem that's causing their passivity. They don't feel in control of their lives so they're letting go of their lives. Parents need to look for what's making their children feel powerless and inadequate. Children need to feel safe and see that their efforts bring about positive results. If a child's self-esteem stays low, parents need to get professional help.

Every parent has those moments when we want to say dreadful

things to our children or spank them. They're natural reactions. It helps, however, when you learn to pull back at these moments and not react. No parent wants to lose control. Being proactive, versus reactive, is a *learned* response. Take time to get your bearings and figure out the best plan of action with your children. A Wedge of Time lets you get away from the situation and gain fresh perspective. After thinking about something else for a while and letting strong emotions subside, you'll be better able to deal with the problem calmly and rationally.

What children need is tender loving care to build and maintain a positive image of themselves. Think about your goal of R=TLC and figure out how you can use tender loving care on yourself as well as your child. The best method is to "catch them being good."

The National Committee to Prevent Child Abuse and Neglect uses the following in a media campaign. The ad shows a little girl listening to the mouths of several angry adults. Here's the dialogue:

> *Have you ever abused your child? Perhaps without realizing it, you have. Words can hit as hard as a fist. For example: "You disgust me." "Just shut up." "Get out of here. I'm sick of looking at your face." "You're pathetic." "Can't you do anything right?" "You're more trouble than you're worth. Why don't you go and find someplace else to live?" "I wish you were never born." Children believe whatever their parents tell them. Next time you lose your temper, stop for a minute, listen to what you're saying. You might not believe your own words. Take time out. Don't take it out on your kid.*

Centuries of tradition have encouraged punishment as a way of controlling children. Today, we want to eliminate this as a parenting method. You now know there are far superior methods of raising children.

❤

CHAPTER TWELVE

CONFLICT RESOLUTION

Conflict occurs when two or more people have differing points of view about a problem. Conflict is perpetuated when people cling tenaciously to their own point of view and refuse to hear other viewpoints. Unfortunately, our point of view gives us tunnel vision. That is, we can see light ahead of us, but nothing at all in the darkness around us. We only have part of the picture. When embroiled in a conflict, our own little picture is all that we know. Being in conflict is a stressful situation in which some of our fundamental needs are not being met.

Literal Thinkers

In order to understand conflict, we need to consider what literal thinkers most of us are. We tend to see the world in opposites. We often polarize our ideas: things are either/or, black or white, me or you. We stay in conflict with others because we think we're right. However, you may only be "right" about the facts as you know them, and you might not have all the facts. The same is true for your opposition. That person has the same tunnel vision problem.

If the stakes are high in a conflict, as in who will have custody of the children and how to divide the assets in a divorce, then the situation can become very messy. Literal thinking may become more pronounced.

Jerry desperately wants to be an active father to his two sons and has been granted regular visitation rights. He also has a legal right to call his boys daily. He pays his child support regularly. Yet, every time he calls his ex-wife's home, the answering machine is on and no one picks up or returns his calls. When he reaches his ex-wife, Nancy, at work, she says that the family was "out." He believes that she's screening her calls and deliberately avoiding him.

Nancy agrees that Jerry can pick up the boys on Saturday morning at 9:00 A.M., but when he arrives, they're still in their pajamas and haven't had breakfast. He fumes as he waits outside. On his last visit, his son asked him, "Daddy, why did you beat up on Mommy?" He was devastated by that remark. "I never beat up on your mother," was his response. When I asked Jerry why he thinks she acts this way, his only response is that "she's crazy."

I've heard countless men call the mothers of their children "crazy." I decided that Jerry doesn't have a clue as to the reason for Nancy's behavior. He's thinking literally: "I'm sane and she's crazy; I'm reasonable and she's unreasonable." Conflict isn't likely to be solved with "I'm right, you're wrong" posturing. The problem is that *both of them are right!*

Try this little exercise that we do in our parenting classes. Make a tight fist, then relax your fingers a bit and look through the opening at something in the room you're in right now. Concentrate on what you see. It might be a leaf on a plant or the ear of a cat. Is what you are looking at "right"? Yes, it's right. Is it "right" about the contents of the whole room (i.e., the big picture)? No, it's not even close.

What happens in many conflicts is that people are so adamant about being right, that they have tunnel vision. Everyone is right, and problems don't get resolved. For example, Jerry isn't likely to achieve his goal of having a good relationship with his sons if better methods of conflict resolution aren't put into play with his ex-wife. He has to stop focusing on making Nancy "wrong" so that he can let more information in and understand the big picture.

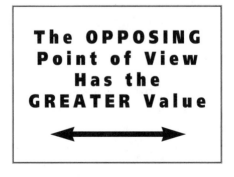

The OPPOSING Point of View Has the GREATER Value

Many problems in our Parent Connection classes have been resolved when parents learn the principle "the opposing point of view has the greater value." It's not that your point of view has no value, but that it tends to be one-sided. When you're in conflict with another person, what's missing is the information that the other person is operating from, their *real* point of view, and not just what they're saying or doing to put you off.

Telling the Truth

When there's conflict, people often avoid telling the complete truth. The main reason is they're afraid to do so. They fear that they'll be blamed for something and that matters will only get worse. Past experience has taught most of us that this is likely to happen. The problem is that if you don't have the whole truth, there's little chance the conflict can be resolved.

Children learn not to tell the truth to avoid being punished. Many times this behavior is reinforced because a parent believes their falsehood and they get away with it. Or they never learned a better way of expressing themselves. Children are often punished when they tell the truth. When Little Joey says, "Yes, Dad, I did set fire to the trash can," instead of being counseled and praised for having the courage to tell the truth, Joey gets a spanking. Joey isn't stupid, so the next time he lies when he does something wrong. What the heck, he may get away with it and avoid punishment. If he gets caught lying, he figures that he'll be punished whether he tells the truth or not.

Think about this. Were you ever punished for telling the truth? Was there a time when you were embarrassed for doing so? Did someone see this as a vulnerability and use it against you? Was your self-esteem lowered? How many times have you fabricated the truth, just to avoid "making things worse"? Little children like Joey grow up to be adults. If no one teaches us a better way, we'll continue to use Joey's way. Plenty of adults do.

When I was a young child, I was a curious observer of the "polite lie" that was common in my family. It didn't seem like anyone ever got a straight answer to a question. I used to wonder, What would happen if everyone had a little round red neon light in the middle of their forehead that would flash every time that person told a lie? Wouldn't the world be a better place if everyone automatically told the truth, even if the other person might not like hearing it? Wouldn't you rather know the truth than a story someone made up which was supposed to be "better" for you? I think that people don't tell the truth because most of them don't know how without becoming vulnerable.

Truth is the Only Way that Conflict Can Ever Be Resolved

All rational thought is based on knowing the truth. No one can make good choices if they're not told the truth. It's the essence of good mental health. Truth is the foundation of reasoning. Yet, many of us have been raised in environments where telling the truth was unsafe. What can we do to get someone we're in conflict with to tell us the truth? Clearly, force and blame won't help.

Nancy doesn't feel safe in telling Jerry the truth. However, there are some facts that we can deduce from her behavior. She acts afraid of Jerry. She doesn't want any contact with him, nor does she want "her" children to be with a person she doesn't feel safe with. She's afraid that he'll harm her and her children. Jerry acts surprised by this analysis. He says that she doesn't have anything to be afraid of. Maybe and maybe not. The point is she's afraid of him, and fear doesn't happen in a vacuum. Something has caused her to believe he's dangerous and to be afraid of him.

Everyone has a Private Logic for Everything They Say and Do

Another important point about conflict: you may not understand another person's logic, but that doesn't mean that logic doesn't exist. Every person has a reason for everything they do. Count on it. People have private logic—private thoughts they aren't willing to share, especially if they don't feel safe.

Receptive Listening

One way to resolve a conflict entails first putting your point of view on the shelf for a while. Let it go. Then listen to the other person. Use receptive listening techniques (being culturally-appropriate) to concentrate on the words said, look the person in the eye, watch and read their body language, listen to their tone of voice, and observe any subtle clues they give off about how they feel and about what and why they feel the way they do. If you're filtering this process through your "yeah, but—" reactions or mentally preparing a counterargument, you're not listening receptively. Let yourself hear the opposing point of view. Let the person talk and talk until they're talked out. Keep listening, even if what you're hearing doesn't feel good. Even if you're being blamed for everything that ever went wrong in the world, hang in there.

Once your child or another family member has said what is on his or her mind, your next job is to check to be sure you've heard the information correctly. Staying calm and polite, say something to the effect of, "I really want to know if I understand what you've just said. Let me know if I've heard you correctly." Then repeat what you think you heard, using your own words but not adding any interpretation, opinions, or judgments. This is a reality check to see if you understand the opposing point of view. You need to feed back three things to the other person: (1) how they *feel*, (2) about *what*, and (3) you tell your reason *why* you think the other person feels the way they do. You'll rarely go wrong if you use this simple formula.

If you didn't understand the other person, you've opened a door to having your perception corrected. If this happens, use the receptive listening formula again. Repeat back what you think you heard. If that person says, "Yes, that's what I mean, or something to that effect," then you've succeeded at getting at the truth. This is a big step. In fact, so few people can do this, that if you can, you've reached a *breakthrough!*

It will help a lot if you "catch them being good." Praise them for their honesty and express your appreciation for it. Take responsibility for anything that was true where there was poor judgment on your part; you may have even forgotten about an incident long ago or thought it was trivial. If appropriate, express your sorrow for causing the other person pain. Now that you understand the other point of view, you would like to make it right.

Now you're ready to ask if you can tell your side of the story as *you* understand it. Since your opposition has been heard, the probability is high that this person will return the favor and listen to your point of view. If you get a "Yes," then proceed in a non-accusing way. If you get a "No," ask for another time to share your viewpoint. Be sensitive as to whether the timing is right to continue. Keep the door open for further discussion. It takes time to mull things over and get a fresh perspective on what you've heard. Conflicts are rarely resolved immediately.

"I" Statements

An excellent way to avoid conflicts or power struggles with your children is to use assertive communication, and assertive communication entails using "I" statements. Tell the other person, "I feel _____ about _____," and explain the reason why you feel that way. Communicating assertively will help you avoid blaming the other person for causing you pain. If you lapse into the "accusatory you," you'll find yourself engaged in a power struggle. You can avoid such a deadlock simply by owning responsibility for your feelings. Here are some key phrases for starting "I" statements:

"When this happened, I felt _____ ."
"I didn't understand that _____ ."
"I was upset by _____ ."
"I was grateful when _____ ."

"I" statements are some of the most powerful sentences you can use in resolving conflict. Jerry initiated an open door process with Nancy when he said, "I am confused about what our son meant when he asked me why I beat up on you. If I knew what he was referring to, I might be able to do something about it."

Can you see the benefits of "the opposing point of view has the greater value"? When you receptively listen to the other point of view, you'll have much more information than when you're stuck in your own tunnel. The process sheds light on why the conflict exists. With the truth, you have a better grasp of the Big Picture. A real breakthrough occurs when you can reframe your perception of the conflict to be more in alignment with what really happened versus your interpretation of what happened. We all tend to come to premature conclusions based on the only information we have. When you have all the facts, your interpretation might change.

Jerry and Nancy are success stories in conflict resolution. They needed an objective third party to sort through their past and help them heal old wounds. They did some post-divorce counseling. I knew Jerry fairly well by the time Nancy came in for a session. She was hardly a "crazy" person. Jerry's well-timed "I" statement made it safe for her to tell the truth about what she was feeling by responding with her own "I" statement. She brought up several situations in their stormy relationship that Jerry had either minimized or forgotten. There had been some problems with Jerry's drinking. Also, Nancy felt that he was too controlling with her and entirely too strict with their children. Also, a fight had occurred with pushing and shoving, and she had been knocked down.

This was a turning point for Nancy, and she began planning a way to leave Jerry. They'd never discussed their problems or had any counseling. She saw no resolution other than a divorce. The judge's decision to give Jerry visitation rights didn't change her feelings that the children would be unsafe with him.

Jerry's point of view was that Nancy was entirely too lenient with the children, and he felt that he had to make up for it. He also thought she was too manipulative. He felt he was made the "heavy" to do the discipline she wouldn't do. She encouraged her parents to interfere. Furthermore, he wasn't treating her or the children any worse than what he had experienced growing up. He admitted that he used to drink too much and that he had lost control and resorted to hitting. Now that he has been to Alcoholics Anonymous, he knows that alcohol doesn't solve problems, but only makes them worse. He pointed out that he had changed his mind about having to be "the boss." He no longer believed that his parents' form of discipline was as good as it could have been. He apologized for past excesses and was sincere in saying that he wanted to share in parenting the boys. A new parenting plan was worked out. The door was open for dialogue, and Jerry and Nancy could now successfully co-parent.

Mothers and fathers typically have different points of view about what each thinks is the right way to parent, and that often leads to conflict. The reason is easy to understand. Each parent was raised in a different family where many values and experiences were not similar. It's a real challenge to work out different approaches to parenting in a new family and in a different era. Attending a parenting class can be helpful in reducing family conflict. In parenting classes, too, couples learn to be more cohesive in their approaches to teaching their children.

Avoiding Power Struggles

People are apt to forget that it takes two to have a power struggle. Avoiding such a struggle doesn't mean giving in—absolutely not! It means forming a different strategy for solving problems. You can say, "This isn't a good time for us to talk about this. When is another time?" Or simply wait. Use time as your ally. When people calm down, they're more likely to be reasonable.

One of the best times to solve problems is *after* a meal. Don't bring up a problem during a meal because it can upset digestion. After people have eaten, however, their blood sugar is stabilized and they're more relaxed. You'll be surprised at how quickly you can solve knotty problems when people have a full stomach.

One of the worst times to work on problems is after a person has had a drink of alcohol or any other intoxicant. If someone is drinking, be sure to pick another time. That was one of the biggest problems that Jerry and Nancy had. Under "the influence," a person's ability to think is distorted and fuzzy. Alcohol alters feelings of empathy and love and, of course, it fuels false confidence, resulting in irresponsible behavior.

Nancy and Jerry both completed their parenting course. They learned to forgive each other. They found increasingly better ways to share in the parenting of their children. I wish everyone in conflict could have a success story like theirs.

The way their conflict was resolved was by applying the principle that "the opposing point of view has the greater value." Once the problem was identified, the logical problem-solving process could proceed. They solved their conflict in a win-win way.

Problem Solving

Solving problems as they arise reduces overall family conflict. As we discussed in Chapter 8, a problem indicates the presence of a need to be met. Remember, the common pattern for all problem solving involves these six steps:

1. *What is the problem?*

2. *Analyze the problem.*

3. *What will solve the problem?*

4. *Make a plan.*

5. *Do it.*

6. *Evaluate.*

Let's see how each of these steps, when put into action, helps resolve family conflict.

1. What is the problem?

Admitting that a problem exists is a critical first step. Have you ever felt that "something" just isn't right, but you can't put your finger on it? Eventually something happens and you identify the problem. Just defining the problem is a big step in solving it. Built into every problem is a solution. Here's an example of how a father solved the problem of getting his daughter up in the morning.

Katherine (10) used to bounce out of bed, ready for the day, but lately she's turned into a zombie in the morning. Her eyes don't open when she gets up, she bumps into things, and if anyone tells her to do anything, she gets irritable. Mornings have become very difficult to handle, because everyone would rather avoid Katherine.

2. Analyze the problem.

You need to probe deeper into a problem to find its solution.

Clearly, Katherine's behavior upsets the whole family. It represents a change from the Katherine they used to know, the child who bounced right out of bed in a good mood. Her behavior makes the whole family late in leaving the house in the morning. What is the *real* problem? Katherine's father started with this analysis:

a. We're late.
b. Katherine is grouchy.
c. No one wants to be around her.

However, these issues are secondary to the real problem. To find this, we must look for the source, or cause, of her behavior. When you analyze the problem and find the cause, you'll have a clear direction for working on the solution.

The key here is that the change in Katherine's behavior is recent. What's wrong with Katherine's energy? She doesn't have the get-up-and-go she needs.

3. What will solve the problem?

Katherine's father thought further about possible solutions to the problem:

a. Is Katherine sick? Should we take her to the doctor for a check-up?
b. Have a talk with her about how unpleasant she is in the morning. Tell her to correct her behavior. (Probable response: "I don't know why I'm like this.")
c. Yell, scream, *wake her up!* (Probable response: "Stop yelling; I hate you." She slams the door and scowls at everyone.)
d. Try a simple experiment of giving her a glass of orange juice when she first wakes up to see if she has low blood sugar in the morning.

Can you think of other possible solutions?

4. Make a plan.

Of the four alternative solutions that Katherine's father came up with, what kind of a plan would *you* make?

Here's what one father suggested in a Parent Connection class. Later in the day, when Katherine is in a good mood, he would first talk to her in a non-threatening way. He would say, "Katherine, everyone in the family is having a problem leaving the house in the morning on time. We need you to help us out more. You used to bounce out of bed with energy and were a big help in getting everyone ready. Now, you seem very tired and irritable. Since you didn't used to be this way, I'm wondering what you think is the cause of the problem."

"I don't know, Dad. I just don't feel like getting up."

"Well, it's something that we have to work on. I wonder what will solve the problem."

This democratic leadership style cleverly involves Katherine in helping solve the problem in a non-threatening way. It uses the principle of *participation* or *negotiation*. It also uses *good timing*, waiting until she's in a good mood to bring up the subject. It could then go on to the second-easiest possible solution on her father's list, that is, give her a glass of orange juice in the morning to see if low blood sugar is the source of the problem.

"Katherine, I suggest that tomorrow when you get up, that you drink a glass of orange juice to see if that will perk you up. If you have low blood sugar, then the orange juice will take care of it. If that doesn't work, we may need to take you to Dr. Lee for a check-up."

Katherine readily agreed. She preferred not to visit the doctor if she could avoid it. The next morning, she drank her orange juice when she woke up. Within a few minutes, she brightened up and started moving out of her zombie state. It was the first time in several weeks that the family had a peaceful morning and got a timely start on their day. Hooray! But is the problem solved? We now know some information that we didn't have before. Katherine is experiencing low blood sugar in the morning. *Why?*

Further discussion between Katherine and her father tracked down the real cause of the problem. Katherine had greatly increased the number of cola drinks, ice cream, and junk food in her diet. She was skipping breakfast. She was using her lunch money for the wrong food. The family also had a huge box of chocolates, a birthday gift, which they had been eating recently. It all added up to a lot of sugary foods. "You are what you eat," the adage goes. Her mother explained to her that the effect of too much sugar caused hypoglycemia, that is, her body over-reacted to large amounts of sugar and gobbled up too much, leaving her with low blood sugar in the morning. Hypoglycemia can warrant a doctor's attention, but the family decided to try their own simple experiment first.

5. Do it.

Together, Mom, Dad, and Katherine made a plan and carried it out: Katherine slowed down on the junk food, ate breakfast, and discussed how she was feeling with her mother and father at the end of the week.

6. Evaluate.

As the week progressed, it was clear that Katherine was making a big effort to solve the problem. Her parents followed through by commenting every morning how much better things were. By the end of the week, they all agreed that the mornings were much more peaceful, and profusely thanked Katherine for her cooperation.

On the next weekend, Katherine was invited to a birthday party. She loaded up on cake, ice cream, coke, and candy. Sure enough, the next morning she was dragging. Everyone was late again. Her parents followed through with another evaluation, much like the first step. "Katherine, we had a problem this morning getting off to work on time. What do you think was the cause of it?" When Katherine put together what she ate at the party the day before with how she felt in the morning, her parents knew that they had been successful in teaching her something important about how to control her moods and energy.

The Joy of Conflict Resolution

When you have a problem, whether it's at work, at play or in a relationship, the Six Steps can help you solve it. The more adept you become at using them, the faster you'll solve problems and head off family conflict. You can turn solving problems into a joyful experience, a chance to grow and deepen relationships. There's such satisfaction in exercising your mind and continuously improving on your ability to get along with others. It's like a great workout for the muscles in your body—it feels *good.*

❤

CHAPTER THIRTEEN
SENSITIVE SUBJECTS

"If you've tried to do something and failed, you're vastly better off than if you've tried to do nothing and succeeded."

—Anonymous

A "sensitive" subject is something that you don't feel comfortable talking about with your children. You're not sure what to say to them. You don't know if you have all the facts. Sometimes you wish someone else would talk to them.

- "How did the baby get inside of that woman's stomach?"
- "Why did Grandpa die? Where did he go?"
- "Mama, why does Uncle Rick get drunk?"
- "Why did that man go to jail?"

Parents feel awkward about different subjects. One father can easily discuss sex, but gets sweaty when he talks about why he got a divorce. Others may feel awkward talking about drug abuse because they don't have good boundaries for themselves (perhaps one martini leads to another, and then to a bottle of wine with dinner). The point is, whatever subject you feel awkward about is likely to be the subject that your child needs to know about...and know about *from you*. A constructive way to read this chapter is to pay attention to what makes you uncomfortable. Make a mental note to strengthen your ability to talk with your children about that subject.

We know that *responsibility* means to *respond appropriately,* to take action, to have the confidence to act when required. It also means being mature enough to be accountable for your choices and to measure up to your obligations and duties. Responsibility means being able to follow though and finish what you begin. In order to be responsible, children (and parents!) must be able to distinguish between what's right and wrong, know what to think, and know when to act. Qualities of a responsible person are being trustworthy, dependable, and reliable. Parents need to be responsible resources for their children.

One of the greatest gifts we can give our children is to teach them to be responsible. We do this by helping them to develop good thinking, to be loving, and to be confident. We need to start early in seeing that they follow through with age-appropriate obligations and duties. Early in life, we teach children to respect property, to pay for damages, to tell the truth, to be cautious about strangers, and to eat healthy food.

Today's children also need to know the *facts* about sensitive subjects and *how you feel* about them. Here are a few of these issues (we'll cover others later in this chapter).

Drugs and Needles. Children should be taught never to use drugs and absolutely never to shoot drugs into their veins with a used needle. Thinking that your adorable, obedient, intelligent children will never be involved with drugs or needle-sharing is the worst kind of denial. And it isn't a matter of whether they will or they won't use drugs or needles. Knowing that common household bleach will sterilize a needle is part of the information that today's children need for their own or their friends' safety.

Condoms, Sex, and Safety. As children approach puberty, they must also see a condom, open the package, handle it, and inflate it. Tell them where it goes and explain that it keeps sperm from entering the vagina and protects against the spread of disease. Explain why and when a condom must be used. Explain what AIDS is, how AIDS is spread, and how important a condom is in preventing its spread (the same holds true for other sexually-transmitted diseases). Whether children need this information at this stage in their lives or not isn't important. Condoms are a part of the information that everyone, especially today's adolescents, need to know.

Tell your children that there is no such thing as "safe sex." There is always a risk—condoms may break, fall off, or be used incorrectly. There is always a chance for diseases to spread and for unwanted pregnancies. The only safe sexual practice is abstinence.

This brings up another sensitive subject, how an adolescent is to manage sexual urges in a way that won't bring harm to themselves or others. You may be adamantly opposed to condoms and expect your child never to consider having sex outside of marriage. Yet, the truth is, an overwhelming number of teenagers experiment with sex. Telling your children what a condom is or giving other information about birth and disease control is just information. Each person decides what to do with the information. However, if your children have no information, important life decisions end up getting made unwittingly. Responsible parents don't want this for their children.

Pregnancy and Drug Use. Teenagers also need to know that whatever mother takes, her unborn baby gets. A pregnant woman must take special care of her health, including good prenatal medical care, and should not smoke, use drugs, or consume alcohol. Teenagers talk about these things, but without accurate information, they're often pooling their ignorance. If you've done your homework and teach your children the basic facts, they'll become leaders in their peer groups.

Respect for Others. Young children need to learn to treat people of the opposite sex respectfully. The pre-teen years are a good time to teach this, because now, briefly, they're turned off by the opposite sex. The rule to teach is that you don't have to like someone, but you do have to treat them with "respect"; that means no aggressive name calling, putting down, attacking, or spreading damaging rumors. These are not loving acts. One of the best times to teach this is when a child has been hurt by someone. As you listen receptively to those feelings, tell your child not to seek revenge. Many children have an aggressive tendency which can be curbed at this stage. Expressing your feelings goes a long way to healing bad thoughts. The Golden Rule ("How would you like to be treated?") and the Universal Rule ("What if everybody did it?") will help you teach the lesson of respect to your children.

Informed children make better choices when they're under pressure. The time in your child's life when you have the most influence is before age 13. The Parent Connection's intervention program in the Los Angeles County Probation Camps showed us that if a child is going to be very irresponsible, it's most likely to start being obvious around age 13. The early teens are when children begin to come under pressure to conform to influences outside the family. If youngsters don't have a strong sense of identity, of "Who I am," and of good family backing, accompanied by positive values to guide them to make good choices, there can be problems. Without strong parental guidance and support, they can be easy marks for sex, unwanted pregnancy, smoking, alcohol and other drugs, dropping out of school, and gangs. Those most likely to influence them will be youngsters who have not had consistent parent support.

A Worst-Case Scenario

Today's grown children may leave home and then, like a boomerang, come back to live with their parents—only they may not come home alone!

Marjorie has one of the saddest stories I've ever heard. She has two adult children and her ten-year-old son, Pete. She had many personal plans and goals, and her life was comfortable. She and Pete got along well. She liked her job. Meanwhile, her daughter Jackie was having a terrible time managing her life. Marjorie resisted her attempts to move back in with her because Jackie had five children. "You have to make a home of your own. It isn't my job to raise your children. It's yours."

One day Jackie called, crying, "The landlord has thrown me out. I've got no place to go." Marjorie said, "Come over, but you've got to find another place right away."

Once Jackie moved in, Marjorie realized that her grown daughter was behaving worse than the children. She would sleep all day, then be irritable and snap at everyone. Worse, she stole money from Marjorie's purse. The sad fact was that Jackie was a crack addict. There was no peace in the house.

Marjorie finally kicked Jackie out and is now raising six children all under the age of ten, a far greater responsibility than she had ever asked for. When she came into class, Marjorie was resentful and thoroughly disgusted. By just being able to talk things out, she was able to find the burden of six children more manageable.

Clear Expectations and Sexual Responsibility

There's no substitute for education about (1) the responsibilities of being a parent; (2) decisions about whether to have sex, with whom and under what situations; (3) what assertive responses to use when your children are pressured by their peers; and (4) birth control. Many parents wait until it's too late.

I have frequently asked parents, "When do you think would be the best time for your child to lose his or her virginity?" The stunned looks this always gets from parents is very funny. Not many parents have thought that far ahead or even considered that it's any of their business. Actually, it's true that your children will decide on this issue for themselves, but don't you think you could help set the stage for this eventuality with some accurate information about what this serious life step could mean?

How can parents prevent a situation like Jackie's? One way is to start early by helping youngsters visualize what a family entails, and understand that they need to wait until they have the capability and confidence of managing their own lives. "No babies until you're ready." Not bringing new babies into this world until they can assume responsibility for themselves and for their babies is one of the basic rules parents must teach. To accomplish this means teaching sexual responsibility. Some parents are in denial about their youngster's sexual activities, while many others assume that their youngsters will be sexually active and that there's nothing they can do about it. Nothing? This is *neglect*.

The Sack of Flour Experiment

One ingenious high school teacher had her students bring a ten pound sack of flour to school and draw a little face on the package. She then assigned each student the job of keeping the sack of flour with them wherever they went, twenty-four hours a day. When this was impossible, they were to arrange for a sitter. At the beginning of the experiment, the assignment was hilarious. However, it soon became a nuisance, and for most of the students, it was quite sobering at the end. Some of the sacks disintegrated, while others developed rips. Some got disgustingly dirty, and only a few survived two weeks in reasonable shape. All of the students learned from the experience that a baby takes much more time and care than a sack of flour. They learned that taking care of a baby isn't just wishful thinking, and that "Oh, I can handle it" is false confidence.

Marjorie hadn't set basic limits with Jackie because she believed that "kids will be kids" and there was nothing to be done about it. Jackie didn't learn appropriate boundaries. Once Jackie was in her teenage years, Marjorie's helplessness was reflected in an out-of-control teenager. It could have been otherwise.

Typically, teenagers feel invincible. They believe that nothing will hurt them, so they minimize the seriousness of their actions. They don't project the consequences of their behavior to their future. Although they may have the facts of life, they still don't believe that having sex tonight can make a baby arrive nine months later. They're just as unrealistic about disease, accidents, and other dangers.

Teenagers take risks. Unsupervised, they're drawn to what looks like fun, but is, in reality, a menacing threat. Falling in love can mean taking a big fall. Several of our adolescents in youth camp describe "playing at being married" experiences. Larissa said that she had been living with her boyfriend for five years. I wondered how this could be. She was only seventeen. I asked, "Where is your mother?" She said, "Oh, she lives with us." I further asked, "Who pays the bills?" "Mom does." Teenagers need to have appropriate roles demonstrated as well as spelled out for them. Larissa and her mother did not have a clear understanding of their roles.

Marjorie was a mother I followed for a few years. She continued coming to the classes for support. She dreamed of the day when Jackie would pull herself together and be able to take responsibility for her own children, but Jackie developed AIDS. Marjorie's difficulties turned into a nightmare. Had Jackie passed the HIV virus on to her children? She had them tested, and to her relief, none of them were HIV positive. I admire Marjorie. She grew to the task of managing six children in her middle years. She learned how abusive and neglectful practices are passed from generation to generation. She was determined to do a better job with her "second chance."

Teenage-Proofing Adolescents

Teaching adolescents about sensitive subjects is critical, just as important as teaching young children not to play with fire. Most parents know about "baby-proofing" a house, but how can you "teenage-proof" an adolescent? The worst way is to wring your hands and do nothing. The best way is with education. Youngsters armed with facts always make better decisions. They anticipate more, are more inclined to see a future for themselves, and are more realistic about living up to their potential. Although they expect obstacles in life, your help will give them ideas about how to get around them. When stuck, they'll talk things over with an interested parent, a kind teacher, a friend, or a relative.

Thinking Ahead

I've already suggested that much of the learning about sensitive subjects should take place by age 13, before the "turbulent teens." Because proactive parents think ahead, so do their children. By age 13, children are capable of knowing that drugs, unprotected sex, AIDS, death, and separation/divorce are part of life. Although they may not understand as adults can, they can absorb valuable knowledge from which they can draw when they need it. As new information comes their way, they make deposits in their knowledge bank, adding to what they already know. As they experience life, it need not be from "the school of hard knocks." Sometimes pain can be prevented with good decisions.

Tammy had an urgent, desperate need to go to a party thrown by questionable friends. If she could have envisioned the consequences—her subsequent drug addiction and slide into juvenile delinquency, her teenage pregnancy, the loss of a college education, lower income power for the rest of her life—she might have been willing to skip the party. Had she known, she might have said, "Mom and Dad, it would have been better for me if you had risked letting me be disappointed temporarily in exchange for a better life."

Can just one party cause all that to happen? It only takes one party to fall in love or to take drugs for the first time. It all starts somewhere. Parents must be attentive to the sort of individuals their children are associating with during their teenage years when they're especially vulnerable to peer pressure. Many parents are confused into thinking that what youngsters want must be what's good for them. If adolescents knew better, they wouldn't want to expose themselves to such risks. But they don't know better unless they've had firm guidance by proactive parents.

When Do Children Go Astray?

Problems can start very early, but youngsters first begin to act on their desires around 13 or at puberty. I've asked several juvenile delinquents when they first got in trouble with the law.

Darlene said she was 13 when she started smoking pot and running with her neighborhood gang. She claimed that the cause of this behavior was a change in schools. She said, "I was in a private school and then I started in a public junior high. That's when I started to get crazy—skip school, start drinking, and not listen to my mother."

I wasn't satisfied with her explanation, so I probed further as to why leaving a private school for public school would make her end up in jail. What else was happening at that time? She told me that she and her mother, Patty, had been very close. When Darlene was 11, her mother fell in love again, and Earl, her new boyfriend, got all Mom's attention. Mom suddenly got very busy. The long talks, shopping trips, and outings came to an abrupt stop.

Instead of being angry at her mother, Darlene focused on hating Earl. She refused to speak to him. Whenever he was around, she would walk out of the house. Since she didn't know how to get her mother back, she found comfort in a new family, the V13 Gang. The drugs she was introduced to altered her thinking and her values. She became sexually active and started shoplifting and skipping school.

I interviewed her mother, Patty, a delicate and soft-spoken lady. She told me that she tried talking to Darlene about going back to school and changing friends, but Darlene wouldn't listen. She would just walk out. There was no stopping her until she got arrested for shoplifting. Then, the legal nightmare began.

Darlene was a literal thinker. It was too painful for her to blame her mother for her lack of attention and sense of abandonment. All of the blame went to Earl. Five years later when I first met her in a probation camp, she held the same position. Once Darlene had boyfriends of her own she began to understand and finally to accept that her mother deserved to have companionship in her life.

If Patty had been more open with Darlene early on and prepared Darlene for the possibility of a new man in her life, Darlene wouldn't have felt like the bottom had fallen out of her life. When parents develop warm feelings for a significant other, their children may feel abandoned, as Darlene did. Patty also made the mistake of not paying enough attention to Darlene at this vulnerable time. With more care in making a smooth transition, using assertive communication techniques and addressing self-esteem issues directly, Darlene might have adjusted. Darlene might not have liked the change, but she probably wouldn't have thrown her life into chaos.

If Patty had known the following guidelines for talking to Darlene about sensitive subjects, the story would be different.

Discussion Guidelines

1. Tell the truth. It's never too early to give children facts. Fanciful stories about cute babies delivered by storks, Santa Claus, the Tooth Fairy, and the Easter Bunny can be fun. But children need to know where babies *really* come from. Start early by using the correct words. Call a penis a penis, and call a vagina a vagina. Special picture books make explaining anatomy easier, too.

Animals provide logical opportunities to teach reproduction. Having pets like dogs, cats, and hamsters can help children become accustomed to reproduction. When children see animals mating, explain to them that this is how they make babies. Numerous wonderful books on sensitive subjects are available, too. Picture an author deliberating over each word until it's just right. Imagine the artist or photographer deciding what pictures are best to get the ideas across. Books provide a valuable shortcut for parents. Go to your local library and ask the children's librarian for assistance in finding the right book for your child's age. When I did this, I was unable to carry home all the books the librarian found on reproduction alone. There's a book for every age child on almost every subject, from drugs to AIDS.

If you start early enough, your children will talk about these subjects naturally. They'll feel safe asking you questions. You've given them permission to ask for information. They don't have to be ignorant. Instead, they can build on their knowledge. For instance, I don't recommend giving children one big presentation on "the birds and the bees." If you're doing your job, your child will be acquiring knowledge as he or she grows up. There won't be one big surprise talk on where babies come from.

It is also important to discuss your values with your children. Do you believe that couples should have babies only when they're married and/or financially solvent? Are teenage pregnancies acceptable to you? When is a good time to become sexually active? When is masturbation okay? What are your values about education and how does that fit in with a sexually-active teenager? Is homosexuality a matter of natural orientation, something to hide, or evil and disgusting? Your children need to know your point of view. As they grow up, they'll decide for themselves, regardless of what you think, but they'll have your values to fall back on until they're clear about their own. A parent has reached breakthrough when he or she is able to tell a child, "The choice is yours. You do not have to agree with the way I believe for me to love you." Your job is to influence your children so that they will make responsible value choices.

2. Open the door. The second guideline is to open the door for children to subjects that are sensitive now or could be in the future. "Where do pets go when they die?" "Why do people have to die?" "Will I die?" If you aren't sure how to answer these questions, start preparing. What you say will have a lasting impact.

"What is a homosexual?" "What does she mean when she says, 'I'm a lesbian?'" "What is an abortion?" "Why are people so uptight about whether abortions should be legal?" "Who is the Ku Klux Klan?" "Why is there war?" "Why can't people agree and not fight or kill each other?"

"When is using drugs abuse?" "Is Uncle John an alcoholic?" "Why are Aunt Tilly's children in foster care?" "Why are there homeless people?" "Where do homeless people live if they don't have a home?" "What's wrong with that man who stares off into space and talks to himself?" These are the kinds of questions that children think of, but there are some subjects children won't think of.

When I presented this guideline in one of my classes, a student named Andy told me, "My son is 17. I've never talked with him about sex. I think that even if it's late, that I will bring up the subject." I agreed that opening the door to talking about this, or any other, sensitive subject is valuable—even for older children.

3. Bring up the subject if your child doesn't. What is a pedophile? incest? rape? When is it okay for someone else to touch your private parts— how and for what purpose? to clean them? a physician? a stranger, neighbor, or relative? Tell children that pedophiles are very smooth talkers; they're creative. They're rarely the weird-looking guy who pulls up by the curb and asks, "Do you want to go for a ride?" They can be found where children hang out. They may be coaches, teachers, or members of the clergy. They look perfectly reputable. They're charming; they know the right things to say to children. They may be hard working, caring, and giving. They may be like the rest of us, yet they're sexually aroused by children and may act on their impulses inappropriately.

How are you going to protect your children from a pedophile? It is not enough to tell children not to talk to strangers or get into strangers' cars. The overwhelming majority of child molestation cases are perpetrated by a "friend" or a family member, someone the child already knows. Until the pedophile behaves inappropriately, no one suspects any danger. It's better to warn and to continuously explain, "No one has a right to touch your private parts unless you say so. Your body belongs to you." Now, there are exceptions. For example, a doctor or a parent. But what if these people aren't behaving appropriately? Teach your child to *tell* a trusted grown-up and keep no secrets about uncomfortable touching. Keep the door open. "If someone touches you and it doesn't feel right to you, tell me or tell someone you trust." Also, explain that the police help people who are in danger and show them how to call the police. They can also call 911 or your local emergency hotline.

4. Keep what you say appropriate to the age of your child. Young children can only absorb a small amount of information at a time. Some information needs to be repeated several times. Knowledge is expansive; you'll continue to add to what they've already learned. What you say to a boy-crazy 14-year-old girl about AIDS is very different from what you say to a five-year-old child hearing the term for the first time. Don't offer more than a child can absorb at one time.

5. *Use good timing.* When a child asks for information, it's generally a good time to discuss a sensitive subject. Of course, if a child asks where babies come from when you have the boss over for dinner, you'll promise an explanation later. Set a time to discuss the subject when you feel comfortable, but try not to let too much time go by. Also, make sure that the child is ready to receive the information you want to give. Two people have to be ready to communicate, not just one.

Since I didn't have the advantage of teaching my children when they were very young, they were very resistant to having these talks, especially about sex. Robert continued to say, "Sex is dirty." TJ wouldn't talk about it at all. I bought five books on sexuality for adolescents. I handed them to TJ and said, "These are for you." He looked at me funny, shrugged his shoulders, and put them on the top shelf of his bookcase.

A year and a half later, he and several neighborhood boys ran into his room. They were strangely silent. I could hardly resist not opening the door to see what they were up to. About twenty minutes later, the door burst open and they ran down the block talking excitedly. What was that all about? I wondered. When I went into TJ's room, the five books were all over. From that day on, he read them with great interest. I bought him more books. Soon, the "ice" was broken and we could have discussions about the sensitive subject of sex.

An Important Part of Parenting

Good luck! Remember to use receptive listening when your children express their views and feelings, and use "I" statements when you express your own. Whenever appropriate, share your values on sensitive topics. It's a tough job, but you have to do it. You'll always be grateful that you opened the door to discussing sensitive subjects.

❤

CHAPTER FOURTEEN

THE
GOOD LIFE

No one has children because they want to be miserable! If this is so, why are so many people feeling like they're trapped in family relationships. Why is there so much dysfunction? Why is there so little peace of mind?

Everyone wants to live a good life, a life where you are supported in loving ways, treated with dignity, and respected by others who behave responsibly. Most people realize that having a strong family is an important part of this life. We know that we pass on our heritage through our children. They're our future.

With *Breakthrough Parenting: Unlock the Secrets to a Great Relationship With Your Children*, and its attendant tools and tips, we know how to build that future.

As the twentieth century draws to a close, more people are realizing that there's an opportunity for a fresh start. While this possibility has always existed, the millennium gives the idea momentum.

By reading this book, you've shown that you're ready to leave the old thinking that has limited so many and make a fresh start at the Good Life. You have an opportunity to build a family life that's truly a pleasure. You can apply the formula of R=TLC to your day-to-day affairs, and make a long-term difference in the quality of life for you and your children.

One of the most important messages of this book is that a weak person cannot be a strong parent. The more you develop the qualities of R=TLC, the more successful a parent you'll be.

Peace of Mind

Peace of mind is the foremost quality of the Good Life, and we have peace of mind when our survival needs are being met in a predictable way. Knowing that we're responding appropriately to people and events around us gives us peace of mind, too.

The Good Life is represented in our formula R=TLC, which implies making responsible choices that come from a sound mind, a loving heart, and the confidence to take action when we need to. Peace of mind means being at ease with our lives, knowing that our choices can make a difference and trusting in our ability to choose well.

Peace also implies balance. We experience balance when we're spiritually grounded and have loving relationships with our family, friends and community, all of which help each other achieve the Good Life. A community is a group of individuals who are supportive of each others' goals and are able to share resources for the good of all. Rugged individualism is "out." Being a team player, a contributing member, and a dependable person is "in."

Balance comes from a healthy ego. We can help others without losing sight of the fact that "I am lovable and worthy and deserve to be treated with respect and dignity." A healthy ego allows us to practice the principle of The Golden Rule, treating others the way that we would like to be treated.

We Attract What We Project

"Where Attention Goes, Energy Flows and Results Show."

The only way to live a Good Life is to focus on what is good. We attract what we project. Too many people are stuck worrying about being miserable, therefore they attract misery.

When Sharon introduced herself to the Parent Connection class, she described her son Jason (5) as a "holy terror...he's really bad." In fact there's nothing about Jason that Sharon seemed to like. Jason had been kicked out of *preschool* twice. Her job was in jeopardy because she had to leave work to take him home from school.

Sharon was unable to conceive that Jason could be a joy to be around. Therefore, she didn't believe it. Napoleon Hill, author of *Think and Grow Rich*, was one of the first authors to point out the connection between our thoughts and their results. He said, "What you can conceive and believe, you can achieve." If you can conceive of yourself living a Good Life and believe it, then you can achieve it and have a great relationship with your childrens. Sharon was not able to conceive of Jason as being a joy to be around, a child that she could be proud of. When she thinks of him as a "holy terror," she believes it and her thoughts are achieved.

The solution? First, repair Sharon's self-esteem. Help her to see that she has a victim's personality. No matter what, she cannot win. To her, Jason is living proof of the "I can't win" belief system. We tend to project onto others a mirror image of the person we see inside ourselves. I helped her to see that Jason was "normal"; he was behaving according to how he had been taught. It's a self-fulfilling prophesy. If she wanted something different from Jason, she'd have to change herself *first*. She was putting all of her attention on his needing to change, not realizing that it's her behavior and thoughts that had created the situation. This is another example of how the "I am right" attitude gets parents into conflict with their children.

The way that we label our children has a profound impact on how they will develop. Do you see this connection? It's very important to understand why so many families are unhealthy. Many times it's the parent who is promoting the disease. Families don't function not because they can't function, but because of the way family members think about themselves and each other. It took some time to get Sharon to really understand what was happening. But the end result was that Jason did a 180-degree turn. She learned to make liberal use of "catch him being good!"

Fix the parent and the child is transformed—it is *magic*. Parents are the most important role models that children will ever have. They're far more inclined to do what we do than they are to do what we say.

Feeling guilt, shame, like a victim, abused, neglected, punished, spoiled, and fearful is a choice. It's our bad habits, and our bad thoughts, that make us poor. If you aren't happy, consider how you make yourself unhappy. Stop thinking that other people make you unhappy. *You make you unhappy!* Abraham Lincoln said, "People are about as happy as they make up their minds to be." You can just as easily develop the good habits of noticing where there is family harmony, pointing out when children are being responsible, admiring good thinking, demonstrating acceptance, or showing affection and approval. Replace despair with hope. Lovingly demonstrate to your children what you know about the Good Life. Show them that you know how to be happy, especially with them.

A good family life happens when parents and children cultivate the natural harmony that always exists. A bad family life happens when people cultivate discord. It's all in your point of view. The Good Life is an exquisite give-and-take—the dance of life—moving forward and backward in ways that maximize pleasure, joy, and satisfaction for all members of your family.

Fateful Choices

Life offers us numerous fateful choices. A fateful choice is one where our destiny is forever affected. Afterward, there's no turning back. These decisions affect our fate and the quality of life we'll have. Fateful choices define our lives and forecast our future.

You made fateful choices when you decided on how much education to pursue, on what career path to follow, whether to marry, and whether to have children (how many and when). Other key decisions that you've made are your religious beliefs, your sexual interests and partners, also where to live, and whether to be rich or poor or to have just enough to get by. You've also chosen whether to live a healthful lifestyle and this decision, in most instances, determines how long you'll live. Having made your choices, you're living with the results. The more you take charge of your fateful choices, the happier you'll be, and the happier your family will be.

You Cannot Choose Not to Choose

Everyone makes fateful choices that will affect their lives forever. *You cannot choose not to choose.* The Tablet of Life is written on regardless of whether you do it consciously. You can choose to be undecided, but by default, you've chosen to allow someone else to make decisions for you. One of the scariest choices is to let someone else decide your fate. If you don't like the results and blame others for what happens to you, then you're positioning yourself as a victim.

The Victim

Too many people select a martyr's lifestyle. These victimized individuals invite unhappiness, when they could choose otherwise. Untold numbers of people are like this. Something bad is always happening to them. They're addicted to being negative—no different from an alcoholic or a compulsive overeater or gambler.

Victims respond in a repetitious way to events and end up with the same outcome—more misery. They tend to stay stuck in negative behavior, sometimes for a lifetime. Their common characteristic is blaming others for their "bad luck."

They don't know how to release it and let go. They have a hard time accepting and forgiving. Frequently, they don't see with empathy or sympathy, identifying with the other person's point of view. They're too busy justifying their own viewpoint.

It takes a lot to get the victim's personality to change. They begin to learn to live their lives intentionally. People can actively choose *not* to be victims. They can learn to alter their responses to people who abuse them, and eventually eliminate the entire problem once they have the confidence to do it. Attracting happiness, harmony, cooperation, prosperity, and abundance requires looking for it. There is great value in investing in yourself and in your family by seeking professional counseling. Skilled counselors can help you to heal the past and to refocus your attention on what is a good life for you. I am forever grateful to those people who counseled me during difficult times, and to those who worked with my family to find a better way of living together.

Steve, a parent in one of my classes, is a prime example of someone moving beyond victimhood. Steve's life was in chaos. In our counseling sessions he went into great detail about what a horrible childhood he had. He described very negligent parents. His brothers and sisters treated him badly. "They still do," he complained. One day he told me, "My childhood ruined me!"

I decided to use a different tactic with him. I told him to affirm, "I had a great childhood. My parents loved me. I really had fun when I was a child." He thought this was a strange assignment, but he did it. Whenever negative thoughts came up about his family, he said he affirmed something positive. The next week, he said, "You know, once my dad took me on a fishing trip for the weekend. It was just us. We had so much fun. I wished it could be like that all the time."

After several weeks of positive family affirmations, more and more happy memories of his parents, brothers, and sisters started to flood his awareness. There were many good times, as well as special efforts to help him which he took for granted. He began to get a more balanced picture of his childhood, no longer saying, "My childhood ruined me!"

In the family, a victim or a martyr doesn't take charge or make positive changes because this person is too busy concentrating on the bad things that have happened, are happening, or will happen. He or she is a master of the Blame Game, pointing the finger at their parents, spouse, children, or even the stars or the cards or numerology. As these people see it, something *external* to them is creating the negativity in their lives. They don't see that their own negative mind and their lack of action are the real culprits until they begin to acknowledge that real events are the result of the choices they have made. Again, it may take professional help to make this breakthrough.

How Much Time Have You Spent Planning Your Life?

Have you spent more time planning your vacations than planning your life? Many people don't even bother to set goals and work towards them. They're adrift in a sea of despair because they don't have a clear vision of what is possible for them. "Life is what happens when you are making other plans," John Lennon said. The other plans I think he was referring to were: "Some day in the future, certainly not now, I'll relax, I'll have fun, and I'll enjoy myself."

Do you make yourself unhappy because your family is interfering with what you "really" want to do with your life? Juanita said, "I really wanted to be a lawyer. I've worked twenty years in the post office." Jerry said, "I really wanted to be a mountain climber. I had great plans to climb Mt. Whitney." Jack said, "I dropped out in high school. I was angry at everybody and everything. I would have lived a better life if I'd finished high school. I can't even go to my class reunion."

These people, and countless more, have postponed a Good Life because they had a family. Self-sacrifice is not a virtue. Of course you'll make sacrifices when you're a parent, but that doesn't mean that what you find challenging and most interesting has to be lost to you forever. People are now living 50% longer than they were at the beginning of the twentieth century. Maybe you'd better make some plans. By the way, have you heard the saying, "If I had known that I would live this long, I would have taken better care of myself"? How well are you taking care of yourself?

If You Don't Learn the Lesson the First Time, It Gets Harder

People repeat the same lesson over and over until they learn it. If you don't learn life's lessons the first time, they become harder. "Self sacrifice is not a virtue" is one of these lessons. "Pain is part of life—but you choose to suffer." This is another. Pain provides us with an opportunity to grow. The only answer to, "Why has this negativity happened to me?" is, "So that you can grow, and so that you can learn to make choices that will give you more pleasure than pain." That is what is being responsible. That is R=TLC.

The Absolute Killer of the Good Life

There's no greater mistake than to indulge in negative thinking, continuously seeing what's wrong, instead of what's right. Negativity is the absolute killer of the Good Life. Negativity creates an unhappy, lackluster life of never having enough. It's a self-fulfilling prophesy.

If you feel that your life is a mess, you can turn it completely around by simply changing your focus. Look for what's good—like the good things your children do every day—and build on that. This is your strength. When something bad happens, change it. Grow from the experience. When life hands you a lemon, make a delicious drink out of it. Be creative!

Some of our most important choices are what we believe. Our beliefs *cause* our feelings. Suppose you had never heard that a snake could harm you. If someone held a snake up to you, you wouldn't feel fear because you wouldn't have a belief that causes the fear.

Parents who believe that there's something wrong with them or with their children live in fear. Their belief *causes* the fear. For them, the other shoe is always about to drop, the glass is half empty, and the manure heap has no pony. Their fear and misery spreads from person to person like the common cold. Positive feelings, however, can spread just as easily. It all depends on where you put your attention as a good, responsible, nurturing parent.

There are those who choose to believe that life is good and positive and those who choose to believe that life is bad and negative. And many slide through life trying not to decide. These are the people who let others make their choices for them because they lack the confidence to take charge of their own life and their own fate.

Every Day is a New Beginning

Your goal is to learn how to create happiness wherever you are. Cultivate what feels good to you. If you're experiencing more pain than pleasure, then you need to *do* something about it. The best strategy is to take a Wedge of Time and think about what to do in your situation.

We all know what feels good; the problem is that too few people know how to structure their lives so they experience feeling good with regularity. Remember the adage that every day is a new beginning. You can turn away from negative self-defeating beliefs and behaviors today and cultivate the positive habits of seeing the good that is all around you, especially in your children. Learn to let go of what really doesn't matter. Stop resisting the bad and go for the gold!

A Crisis is Opportunity on the Wings of Danger

The Chinese character for crisis depicts opportunity on the wings of danger. As many parents with problems have learned, a crisis can open new doors. They learn to be better parents, and in so doing, learn to live more responsible, fuller, and more pleasurable lives on all levels. A crisis can help people adjust to their mistakes and plan a better way to live, so that pain is minimized and pleasure maximized. A crisis can open the door to learning more about how to live the Good Life.

I've written about a broad goal of R=TLC that forms a conceptual measuring stick of the Good Life. Considerable research has shown that people who are goal-oriented have more satisfying lives. This is true for many reasons. When you start out on a journey, you plan a strategy of how to get there. If you don't know where you're going, then any road will take you there.

It makes sense to plan your life journey. And this is a journey you'll share with your children. You can build balance into your life and the life of your children by routinely attending to your family, physical, emotional, financial, community, fun, dream, and spiritual goals. Write them down. Talk about them with your children and let them see you continue to grow. You'll be more likely to enjoy the journey together. The Good Life deserves to be shared.

Time for Breakthrough Parenting!

Are you keeping yourself strong mentally and physically? Are you being a powerful role model for your children? Do you avoid self-sacrifice?

The Good Life means being free to choose and being respectful of others' choices. This entails being tolerant and flexible. Do you work harder toward understanding more than you do judging? Are you continuously learning, determined to substitute good habits for bad? Or are you waiting to improve yourself, postponing your dreams for a better day, sometime when you'll have less stress, aren't so busy, or are more financially secure?

Are you quick to count your blessings? Do you delight in "catching others being good"? Is life a pleasure? Are you glad to be alive? If most of your answers are positive and self-affirming, then you're actively choosing the Good Life. You have the uncommon characteristic of celebrating life *now*, and that's what a great family life is all about.

❤